a globalizing world?

AN INTRODUCTION TO THE SOCIAL SCIENCES: UNDERSTANDING SOCIAL CHANGE

This book is part of a series produced in association with The Open University. The complete list of books in the series is as follows:

Questioning Identity: Gender, Class, Ethnicity
edited by Kath Woodward

The Natural and the Social: Uncertainty, Risk, Change
edited by Steve Hinchliffe and Kath Woodward

Ordering Lives: Family, Work and Welfare
edited by Gordon Hughes and Ross Fergusson

A Globalizing World? Culture, Economics, Politics
edited by David Held

Knowledge and the Social Sciences: Theory, Method, Practice
edited by David Goldblatt

The books form part of the Open University courses DD100 and DD121/ DD122 *An Introduction to the Social Sciences: Understanding Social Change.* Details of these and other Open University courses can be obtained from the Course Information and Advice Centre, PO Box 724, The Open University, Milton Keynes MK7 6ZS, United Kingdom: tel. +44 (0)1908 653231, e-mail general-enquiries@open.ac.uk

Alternatively, you may visit the Open University website at http://www.open.ac.uk where you can learn more about the wide range of courses and packs offered at all levels by The Open University.

For availability of other course components visit the webshop at www.ouw.co.uk, or contact Open University Worldwide, Michael Young Building, Walton Hall, Milton Keynes MK7 6AA, United Kingdom for a brochure. tel. +44 (0)1908 858785; fax +44 (0)1908 858787; e-mail ouwenq@open.ac.uk

a globalizing world?
culture, economics, politics

edited by david held

London and New York

in association with

The Open University

First published 2000 by Routledge; written and produced by The Open University
Second edition 2004
11 New Fetter Lane, London EC4P 4EE

Simultaneously published in the USA and Canada by Routledge
29 West 35th Street, New York, NY 10001

Routledge is an imprint of the Taylor & Francis Group

© 2000, 2004 The Open University

This text has been printed on paper produced in Sweden from wood from managed forests using an elemental chlorine-free bleaching process. It has been stated as being environmentally friendly by the Swedish Association for the Protection of Nature.

Edited, designed and typeset by The Open University.

Printed and bound in Malta by Gutenberg Press Limited.

British Library Cataloguing in Publication Data
A catalogue record for this book is available from The British Library

Library of Congress Cataloging in Publication Data
A catalogue record for this book has been requested

ISBN 0-415-32973-6 (hbk)

ISBN 0-415-32974-4 (pbk)

ISBN 0-203-39219-1 (ebk)

2.3

Contents

The Open University course team

John Allen, *Professor of Geography*

Penny Bennett, *Editor*

Pam Berry, *Compositor*

Simon Bromley, *Senior Lecturer in Government*

Lydia Chant, *Course Manager*

Stephen Clift, *Editor*

Allan Cochrane, *Professor of Public Policy*

Lene Connolly, *Print Buying Controller*

Jonathan Davies, *Graphic Designer*

Graham Dawson, *Lecturer in Economics*

Ross Fergusson, *Staff Tutor in Social Policy*

Fran Ford, *Senior Course Co-ordination Secretary*

Ian Fribbance, *Staff Tutor in Economics*

David Goldblatt, *Co-Course Team Chair*

Richard Golden, *Production and Presentation Administrator*

Jenny Gove, *Lecturer in Psychology*

Peter Hamilton, *Lecturer in Sociology*

Celia Hart, *Picture Researcher*

David Held, *Professor of Politics and Sociology*

Susan Himmelweit, *Professor of Economics*

Stephen Hinchliffe, *Lecturer in Geography*

Wendy Hollway, *Professor of Psychology*

Gordon Hughes, *Senior Lecturer in Social Policy*

Wendy Humphreys, *Staff Tutor in Government*

Jonathan Hunt, *Co-publishing Advisor*

Christina Janoszka, *Course Manager*

Pat Jess, *Staff Tutor in Geography*

Bob Kelly, *Staff Tutor in Government*

Margaret Kiloh, *Staff Tutor in Social Policy*

Sylvia Lay-Flurrie, *Secretary*

Gail Lewis, *Senior Lecturer in Social Policy*

Siân Lewis, *Graphic Designer*

Liz McFall, *Lecturer in Sociology*

Tony McGrew, *Professor of International Relations, University of Southampton*

Hugh Mackay, *Staff Tutor in Sociology*

Maureen Mackintosh, *Professor of Economics*

Eugene McLaughlin, *Senior Lecturer in Criminology and Social Policy*

Andrew Metcalf, *Senior Producer, BBC*

Gerry Mooney, *Staff Tutor in Social Policy*

Lesley Moore, *Senior Course Co-ordination Secretary*

Ray Munns, *Graphic Artist*

Karim Murji, *Senior Lecturer in Sociology*

Sarah Neal, *Lecturer in Social Policy*

Kathy Pain, *Staff Tutor in Geography*

Clive Pearson, *Tutor Panel*

Ann Phoenix, *Professor of Psychology*

Lynn Poole, *Tutor Panel*

Raia Prokhovnik, *Senior Lecturer in Government*

Norma Sherratt, *Staff Tutor in Sociology*

Roberto Simonetti, *Lecturer in Economics*

Dick Skellington, *Project Officer*

Brenda Smith, *Staff Tutor in Psychology*

Mark Smith, *Senior Lecturer in Government*

Matt Staples, *Course Manager*

Grahame Thompson, *Professor of Political Economy*

Ken Thompson, *Professor of Sociology*

Diane Watson, *Staff Tutor in Sociology*

Stuart Watt, *Lecturer in Psychology*

Andy Whitehead, *Graphic Artist*

Kath Woodward, *Course Team Chair, Senior Lecturer in Sociology*

Chris Wooldridge, *Editor*

External Assessor

Nigel Thrift, *Professor of Geography, University of Oxford*

Series preface

A Globalizing World? Culture, Economics, Politics is the fourth in a series of five books, entitled *An Introduction to the Social Sciences: Understanding Social Change*. If the social sciences are to retain and extend their relevance in the twenty-first century there can be little doubt that they will have to help us understand social change. In the 1990s an introductory course to the social sciences would have looked completely different.

From a global perspective it appears that the pace of change is quickening, social and political ideas and institutions are under threat. The international landscape has changed; an intensification of technological change across computing, telecommunications, genetics and biotechnology present new political, cultural and moral dilemmas and opportunities. Real intimations of a global environmental crisis in the making have emerged. We are, it appears, living in an uncertain world. We are in new territory.

The same is also true of more local concerns. At the beginning of the twenty-first century both societies and the social sciences are in a state of flux. *Understanding Social Change* has been written at a moment that reflects, albeit in a partial way, subterranean shifts in the social and cultural character of the UK. Established social divisions and social identities of class, gender, ethnicity and nation are fragmenting and re-forming. Core institutions such as the family, work and welfare have become more diverse and complex. It is also a moment when significant processes of change have been set in train – such as constitutional reform and European economic and monetary union – whose longer-term trajectory remains uncertain. The flux in the social sciences has been tumultuous. Social change, uncertainty and diversity have rendered many of the most well-established frameworks in the social sciences of limited use and value. Social change on this scale demands fresh perspectives and new systems of explanation.

In this context *Understanding Social Change* is part of a bold and innovative educational project, for it attempts to capture and explore these processes of momentous social change and in doing so reasserts the utility and necessity of the social sciences. Each of the five books which make up the series attempts precisely this, and they all do so from a fundamentally interdisciplinary perspective. Social change is no respecter of the boundaries of disciplines and the tidy boxes that social scientists have often tried to squeeze it into. Above all, *Understanding Social Change* seeks to maintain and extend the Open University's democratic educational mission: to reach and enthuse an enormously diverse student population; to insist that critical, informed, reflexive engagement with the direction of social change is not a matter for elites and professional social scientists alone.

As you may have guessed, this series of books forms a core component of the Open University, Faculty of Social Sciences, level 1 course, DD100 *An Introduction to the Social Sciences: Understanding Social Change*. Each book in the series can be read independently of the other books and independently from the rest of the materials that make up the Open University course. However, if you wish to use the series as a whole, there are a number of references to chapters in other books in the series, and these are easily identifiable because they are printed in bold type.

Making the course and these books has been a long and complex process, and thanks are due to an enormous number of people.

First and foremost, the entire project has been managed and kept on the rails, when it was in mortal danger of flying off them, by our excellent Course Manager, Christina Janoszka. In the DD100 office, Fran Ford, Lesley Moore and Sylvia Lay-Flurrie have been the calm eye at the centre of a turbulent storm, our thanks to all of them. For the second edition we have had the much valued support of Matt Staples and Lydia Chant.

Stephen Clift, Chris Wooldridge and Penny Bennett have been meticulous, hawk-eyed editors. Siân Lewis has provided superb design work, and Ray Munns and Andy Whitehead have provided skilled cartographic and artistic work. David Calderwood and then Richard Golden in project control have arranged and guided the schedule with calm efficiency and Celia Hart has provided great support with illustrations and photographs. Nigel Thrift, our external assessor, and Clive Pearson, Elizabeth Chaplin and Lynne Poole, our tutor panel, provided consistent and focused criticism, support and advice. Peggotty Graham has been an invaluable friend of *Understanding Social Change* and David Held provided balance, perspective and insight as only he can.

It only remains for us to say that we hope you find *Understanding Social Change* an engaging and illuminating introduction to the social sciences, and in turn you find the social sciences essential for understanding life in the twenty-first century.

David Goldblatt
Kath Woodward
Co-Chairs, The Open University Course Team

Introduction

David Held

Consider our planet well before the period of commercial and industrial development. Now imagine yourself in one corner of this planet, living in close collaboration with others – say, in a village or small town – but geographically isolated from other inhabited areas, regions, islands and continents. Your circumstances might be similar to those of a typical occupant of an English village a thousand years ago, for whom the village was practically the beginning and end of his or her world: visitors were rare, few travellers passed by, and excursions from the village would, in all likelihood, have only been to the nearest market town (Laccy and Danziger, 1999). Contact with the outside world would have been by exception rather than by rule. At this time, much of the world was still to be 'discovered' (although it was, of course, home to many peoples). There were no detailed maps dividing the earth into neatly demarcated areas, clearly charted seas and established routes for communications or trade.

In this world, human communities developed in relative isolation, with little contact with one another. They were, as one commentator described the ancient civilizations of China, Japan and Islam, quite 'discrete worlds' (Fernández-Armesto, 1995, Ch. 1). Now consider, with the passage of time and technological changes affecting transport, agriculture and commerce, a steady extension of contact with neighbouring communities. Increasing trade would flow across local areas and, eventually, into larger trading networks extending across land masses and the seas. The economic fortunes of different societies could become linked, creating avenues for the dissemination of ideas and technological innovations. Such developments might have considerable impact on particular societies, partly because of their novelty value, but this world could still be described as a site of relatively isolated populations and territories, albeit now conjoined by developing networks of travel, exploration, military adventurism and trade. The diffusion of ideas, goods and people would largely be concentrated within and across adjacent communities and regions, not yet on a world-wide scale.

For thousands of years, human beings have, of course, travelled – settling new lands, exploring the seas, building empires or searching for the means of subsistence. However, it is important to recall that it is only in the last five hundred years that they have travelled the world, conquering and linking together the Americas and Oceania, Africa and Asia. This explosion of travel, migration, fighting, and economic interchange provided an enormous impetus to the transformation of the form and shape of human communities; for the latter became increasingly enmeshed in networks and systems of interchange – a new era of regional and global movement of people, goods, information and microbes was established. Social, political and economic activities could stretch across communities, regions and continents; increasing proportions of human energy could be devoted to such activities, as flows of trade, investment and culture increased; organizations and mechanisms of power and control (empires, colonization and large corporations) could search the world for advantage; and it became possible for all this to happen much more quickly, as new systems of transportation and communication emerged.

On the back of these developments, new economic, political and cultural infrastructures and organizations developed, making possible a transformation in the spatial organization of social relations and transactions, and generating increased levels of activity across particular communities and, indeed, across the entire world. Today, we have a heightened perception of this; e-mail is sent across the planet in seconds; financial markets stretch across the globe; large multinational corporations dwarf the economies of many countries; jobs often depend on decisions in far-off places; supermarkets are stocked with goods from all over the world; drug-related crime is organized on a transnational basis and some of the most important threats to humankind – global warming, ozone depletion and pollution – escape the jurisdiction of particular states and societies. In short, from the 'age of discovery' to the new millennium, processes of change have been underway that have altered the relations and connections between peoples and communities – processes which have been captured by the term 'globalization'.

This book is about globalization, one of the most talked-about phenomena of the last 20 years. But the term is so often used it is in danger of becoming a cliché. Moreover, its value and utility are subject to intensive debate. Indeed, some cast doubt, on the basis of detailed empirical inquiry, on whether the term globalization offers any real illumination at all. Accordingly, this book sets out to examine the following questions:

1   What is globalization? How should it be conceptualized?

2   How distinctive is contemporary globalization in relation to previous eras?

3   What is the impact of globalization on individual political communities and, in particular, on the sovereignty and autonomy of modern nation-states?

4   Does globalization create new patterns of inequality and stratification – in other words, new patterns of winners and losers?

Clearly, in an introductory volume of this kind, these questions cannot be pursued in great detail and across all the many dimensions of historical change implicated in the debate. Fortunately, an introduction to the debate can be aided by focusing on one set of issues which itself has been at the heart of the discussion of globalization: the prospects of the modern state. The modern world was shaped decisively by the development of political communities tied to particular pieces of land, and formed into nation-states. From the late sixteenth century onward, political power became concentrated in state structures, first in Europe and then, eventually, across the world. Sovereignty, legitimacy and democracy all came to be associated with fixed borders and territories. Against this background, maps could be drawn showing states with clear-cut boundaries and nicely demarcated zones of authority and influence. Today, questions arise as to whether states are still as important as they once were to the organization of human affairs – whether they are, in short, subject to erosion in the wake of globalization.

Three theoretical positions in the literature on globalization can be identified on this issue – globalism, inter-nationalism and transformationalism – and each will be introduced and examined in this volume. Briefly, the globalists argue that we live in an increasingly global age in which states are being subjected to huge economic and political processes of change. These are eroding and fragmenting nation-states and diminishing the power of state managers and personnel. In these circumstances, states are increasingly 'decision takers' and not 'decision makers'. The inter-nationalists strongly resist this view and believe that contemporary global circumstances are not unprecedented. In their account, while there has been an intensification of international and social activity in recent times, this has reinforced and enhanced state powers in many places. For states are building new institutions and responding in all manner of ways to the new challenges ahead. The transformationalists take a different position. They argue that globalization is creating new economic, political and social circumstances which are serving to transform state powers and the context in which states operate. They do not predict the outcome – indeed, it remains uncertain – but believe that politics is no longer, and can no longer be, simply based on nation-states. The socio-spatial context of states is being altered and, along with it, the nature, form and operations of states.

Chapter 1 elaborates these theoretical positions in more detail, while Chapters 2–4 concentrate on examining each position at greater length; all the chapters examine each of the three positions and examines one of them in depth. Chapter 2 includes an exposition of the globalist case, Chapter 3 defends the inter-nationalist position and Chapter 4 advocates transformationalism. These chapters will also unpick some of the major areas of human activity – culture and communications, the economy and politics – which, many argue, are at the centre of processes of globalization (see, for example, Held and McGrew, Goldblatt and Perraton, 1999). Accordingly, the structure of the book is as follows:

- Chapter 1 sets out the concept of globalization and the main theories to be engaged in the book. It also examines innovative ways of mapping the global order.

- Chapter 2 introduces the explosion of communication technologies (broadcasting, the Internet etc.) and examines its implications for networks of power, communities and identities across the globe. The focus is on the ways in which the diffusion of television sustains and empowers global socio-cultural networks, and on how it is appropriated in the production of national and local cultural forms. The chapter evaluates the argument as to whether we are moving to a global information society, and how far the culture industries and the globalization of cultural production (Disney, CNN, Time Warner, Sky, etc.) have changed the dynamics of cultural life.

- Chapter 3 explores the role of international trade, international finance and multinational corporations in the debate about globalization. Important issues in the chapter include the actual extent of globalization in the world economy, the role of global financial institutions, and the problem of whether there has been a shift in the balance of power between nation-states and multinationals. There is also a focus on possible 'winners' and 'losers' from effects associated with globalization.

- Chapter 4 examines the changing role of national governments. It focuses on how politics itself is becoming more global, and the challenge this poses for the interstate system. A key dimension of the 'globalization of politics' is the emergence of forms of global governance. The chapter explores the meaning of this phenomenon and its possibilities and limits. It ends by setting out future possible developments. Could these be towards a corporate world, a technocratic world, a neo-medieval order, or, perhaps, a more democratic world order?

- Finally, a short Afterword brings together some of the themes of the book. It returns to the four key questions which inform the volume and offers tentative responses to them. It also picks up a number of cross-cutting issues which emerge in the chapters: notably, whether or not globalization is unleashing processes and structures that impinge in new ways on the agency (and active choices) of states and societies; and whether or not global processes of change are creating a more diverse and uncertain world marked by new sets of risks and unforeseeable consequences.

Globalization is the buzz-word of our time. Newspapers, radio and television are full of references to it. But social science should only take up this idea if it can be well defended on conceptual, theoretical and empirical grounds: it is the task of this book to help clarify this matter.

References

Fernández-Armesto, F. (1995) *Millennium*, London, Bantam.

Held, D. and McGrew, A., Goldblatt, D. and Perraton, J. (1999) *Global Transformations: Politics, Economics and Culture,* Cambridge, Polity Press.

Lacey, R. and Danziger, D. (1999) *The Year 1000,* London, Little, Brown.

A globalizing society?

Allan Cochrane and Kathy Pain

chapter 1

Contents

1 INTRODUCTION

There is a widely shared – almost taken for granted – view that the world is changing more rapidly and dramatically at the start of the twenty-first century than ever before. Although it may not be a term we all use, many of the changes seem to be associated with something that has been called 'globalization'.

The alleged story of globalization is probably familiar enough and can be told relatively simply. Drugs, crime, sex, war, protest movements, terrorism, disease, people, ideas, images, news, information, entertainment, pollution, goods and money, it is said, now all travel the globe. They are crossing national boundaries and connecting the world on an unprecedented scale and with previously unimaginable speed. The lives of ordinary people everywhere in the world seem increasingly to be shaped by events, decisions and actions that take place far away from where they live and work. Cultures, economies and politics appear to merge across the globe through the rapid exchange of information, ideas and knowledge, and the investment strategies of global corporations.

Some writers suggest that the advent of the mobile phone, satellite television and the Internet means that communication from one side of the globe to the other is virtually instantaneous. Distant events are presented to us on television screens even as they are taking place. Newspaper and TV headlines relay to our homes news of crises, fears and panics, which suggests that across the world change is alarmingly out of control. Many of us fear for our own economic security in the wake of global economic change, while our cultural and political certainties are challenged by the rise of new movements and the emergence of new institutions. The authority of individual nation-states and traditional social institutions seems to be increasingly redundant in the face of powerful and apparently dominant global forces. Even the value of the money in our pockets is dependent on fluctuations in global financial markets.

Again, according to some writers we seem to be living in a world of increasing change and uncertainty, in what Giddens (1999) has characterized as a 'runaway world'. 'For better or worse', he says, 'we are being propelled into a global order that no one fully understands, but which is making its effects felt upon all of us' (Giddens, 1999, Lecture 1).

It is further suggested that the authority of individual nation-states, whose existence and sovereignty has been taken for granted over the past three centuries, is now facing dramatic challenges.

Nation-state
A state which possesses external, fixed, known, demarcated borders, and possesses an internal uniformity of rule.

The key defining characteristics of **nation-states** make them particularly vulnerable in the context of global change, because they are fundamentally defined through their 'supreme jurisdiction over a demarcated territorial area' (Held, 1995, p.49). A key aspect of the nation-state is the precise definition of borders within which it has authority. *States* can be understood as the cluster of institutions which claim ultimate law-making authority over a territory, and claim the monopoly on the legitimate use of coercion and violence. It is the significance of borders that is challenged by the rise of transactions and relationships that cut across borders and either do not accept or simply bypass the old arrangements and the controls associated with them. Nation-states, some argue, are too small to be able to influence global change, and too large to respond effectively to the pressures for increased flexibility and competitiveness, or as Giddens (1999, Lecture 1) put it 'too small to solve the big problems, but also too large to solve the small ones'.

Along with the acceptance of some writers of the notion of globalization – and the belief that it captures something about the ways the world in which we live is currently changing – its existence and meaning remain subjects of intense debate among social scientists. Also debated are questions of 'winners' and 'losers' from globalization, with states, some social classes, gender groups, particular continents and the environment all being identified as possible 'losers'. Some even question whether it represents as significant a break with the past as its more enthusiastic proponents imagine. In this chapter we introduce the main debates about globalization and lay the foundations for the analytical approaches that will be developed in later chapters. We set out to identify the concepts that define globalization and establish criteria to help us decide whether it is a useful way of understanding the nature of contemporary social change. Just because 'globalization' has entered the language, this does not make its meaning any easier to pin down.

2   WHAT IS GLOBALIZATION?

2.1   Some claims

As a starting point in examining some of the social changes that have been associated with the notion of globalization, we will reflect on some of the ways in which the notion has been used to inform contemporary political debates. The extract that follows focuses on some developments in the information technology field that took place in the late 1990s, but it is helpful in highlighting some of the more significant claims that have been made about globalization. In the event the Psion challenge to Microsoft eventually failed as a result of technological advances and the company moved on to other areas of production, but the points raised in the extract remain significant.

ACTIVITY 1.1

First of all, read through the extract overleaf. As you do this, make a note of three or four main points that you feel say something about the nature of global change.

Knocking at Gates's heaven

Psion's telecoms-computer alliance has rocked the Microsoft monolith

Bill Gates is at the centre of a public relations offensive. ...

But even Gates will have his work cut out. For a small British company is at the centre of a fast-growing consortium that could seriously damage Microsoft's control of tomorrow's technology.

In the last week alone the Japanese mobile phone company NTT DoCoMo and the American computer group, Sun Microsystems, have joined Symbian, the consortium led by the palmtop computer manufacturer Psion.

Symbian is a front-runner in the 'wireless' revolution through which the mobile phone is fast being developed to access the Internet, send messages, pay bills and buy shares at speeds up to 40 times faster than today's 'wired' modems. European firms led by the consortium of Psion, Nokia and Ericsson may soon dominate the world market. ...

Psion, run by David Potter, a South African educated at Cambridge, is a minnow by corporate standards. It began making PC games for Sinclair Research in the 1980s before moving into personal organisers and palm-sized computers, where it established a world lead. Recently it linked with Nokia of Finland, Ericsson of Sweden and America's Motorola – who between them control three-quarters of the global market – to form Symbian. Psion's operating system will drive the new 'intelligent' mobile phones.

Microsoft – the world's biggest company in terms of stock market capitalisation – sees the European consortium as a threat to its hold over around 95 per cent of the global software market. The next few years will see a David versus Goliath fight to see whether Windows or Symbian's system dominates.

Most would back the American group, because the size of Microsoft's market lead seems unimpeachable. Gates's company, however, does not have the skills in mobile and telecoms technology Psion and its partners have. But it soon will, at the rate it has been making alliances with other telecoms companies. ...

If anyone had any doubts about where the next phase of the digital highway was leading they were dispelled by the pre-Christmas rush to buy mobile phones. Internet traffic now accounts for 15 per cent of BT's local calls – double the level of a year ago. Experts expect new mobile subscribers to grow at 33 per cent in industrialised nations, compared with 4 per cent for conventional subscribers.

Within five years, sales of mobiles are expected to reach almost 750 million units, or three times the number of PCs. By then, mobile telephony will have overtaken fixed-line connections. It took phones almost 40 years to reach 10 million customers in the US, as against 18 months for web-browsers, according to Professor Gary Hamel of London Business School. ...

Manufacturers know that as more mobile phones are bought they will get cheaper, and generate network effects arising from the fact that the more common they become the more non-users feel the downdraught of exclusion. ...

It is possible to view the world as an invisible blizzard of 1s and 0s speeding through the air at lightning speed, waiting to be repackaged into signals for an array of media including pictures, music, telecoms, print and electronic messages by the next generation of mobiles. In the next few years we will experience a plethora of new products from dozens of manufacturers offering all sorts of services. In the end, the consumer will decide.

But from what products? It could be a lightweight telephone with a compact technology, high-resolution screen, a wristwatch or a palm-held screen with a radio connection possibly to one of the global communication satellite systems already in the process of being established. Digitally encoded data transmitted via satellite will enable anyone to phone or message anyone else instantly, and to access anything on the Internet from the latest football scores to the archives of the Library of Congress. ...

Consumers will no longer have to go shopping, since the shops will simply follow them around, and if they want they could pay for the product or service they are buying from the comfort of a beach in Spain, shifting funds with a computer-phone.

Eventually handheld PCs could be integrated into clothes design, with a microphone woven into a collar, or even a hat. When practically everyone has a discreet phone, there will be no need for a conventional landline telephone in the home. That, of itself, is likely to change the culture of family life, for instance.

The personal market may be the biggest, but corporate demand will be the most profitable. In the US alone, according to Motorola, 40 million employees work nomadically, away from the office, for extended periods. The Columbia Institute for Tele-Information reckons that only 2 per cent of the 9.4 million

square miles of America is 'within four rings of the telephone'. Soon, instant communication will be available to all.

Such commercial opportunities will trigger corporate wars. Last year, 96 per cent of devices surfing the Internet were attached to PCs, nearly all of them running Microsoft's operating system. If Microsoft wants to continue 'ruling' the world the appropriate version of its Windows operating system will have to be installed in mobile devices.

Three months ago Microsoft linked with Qual-comm, a US leader in radio technology, and earlier this year it agreed a joint venture with BT. This is eerily similar to the way in which Gates realised, less than five years ago, that the Internet was going to be big and Microsoft risked being left behind.

Employing huge resources, Gates soon caught up. Hell hath no fury like Microsoft in second place, as the Psion consortium knows too well. Microsoft is determined to ensure that its operating system is stitched into all the major products of the digital age as it moves from the desktop into the mobile world and into web and cable TV. ...

It is because the major mobile phone manufacturers do not want to be strangled by another Microsoft monopoly that they have teamed up with Psion. The aim is to try to establish Psion's Epoc operating system as the industry standard for the new mobile devices before Microsoft carves out a beachhead. They have a 50:50 chance of doing so – and Europe has the chance to catapult itself into a winning position in the information highway race.

Source: *The Guardian*, 20 March 1999

COMMENT

Did you notice the language used to describe the events being reported? What did you think about the messages being conveyed? Phrases such as 'a David versus Goliath fight', 'if Microsoft wants to continue "ruling" the world' and 'strangled by another Microsoft monopoly,' have clear implications. This is the story of a struggle to *dominate* global markets – a story about the power of huge corporate resources and the major influence of just a few key companies and their directors on the ways people communicate globally. This notion of globalization implies the centralization of power in the hands of just a few major organizations (and maybe even individuals). It is consistent with the notion of power as domination (**Allen, 2004**). It emphasizes the role of particular agents in wielding power over others.

The examples used to illustrate the extent and influence of these companies range from the billions of straightforward phone calls that connect people wherever they may be in the world, to the option of picking up the latest football score from a gadget sewn into one's clothing! We are promised a 'hand-held future'. Developments in information and communications technologies have the power to change the *spatial* frames within which we live and work. In other words, they may alter the ways we think about the relations between people and places; they may alter the assumptions that we make about where and when certain activities are permitted or expected to take place. So, instead of having to go to a bank, or visit a broker, we can shift funds about from a beach in Spain; rather than searching for shops, shops will follow customers around electronically. In other words, at least according to these arguments, a new geography is being created within which physical distance is less important than electronic connectedness.

The power expressed through these networks is closer to a more structural understanding in which it is the *institutional* ways of doing things that tend to shape our choices, rather than the demands of any particular social group or agency. It is difficult to see how a single organization could effectively dominate these more complex networks of relations. As Giddens notes, 'In a world based upon active communication ... power that comes only from the top-down loses its edge,' because of 'the need for decentralisation and flexibility' in an 'intrinsically open framework of global communication' (Giddens, 1999, Lecture 5).

The extract conveys a sense that we are, indeed, living in an increasingly global world in which our everyday lives, wherever we live, are shaped by decisions and events over which we have little control. But, at least according to this article, it also looks as if there may actually be scope for individuals to influence major institutions like banks through their use of information and communications technologies. Smaller organizations may be able to challenge the power of globally dominant organizations by forming alliances. Using a global approach, it may be possible for small players to carve out a place in global markets, as in the case of Psion, by forming alliances with larger companies 'who between them control three-quarters of the global market'. This may also have important implications for the way in which the world is governed. Developments in communications technology seem to undermine the political authority of nation-states by posing a threat to national **sovereignty**. Global networks of transnational economic and political power seem to be increasingly important.

Sovereignty
A state's claim to exclusive authority within its boundaries.

2.2   Interpreting globalization

Studying the case of Psion's challenge to Microsoft has helped us begin to build a picture of some of the changes that are typically associated with globalization – but it is still a partial and contested one.

ACTIVITY 1.2

In the following short readings, four writers identify some of the features they associate with a globalizing world at the end of the twentieth century. As you read, try to identify the similarities and differences in the views expressed by the four authors. How do their claims fit with your own experience?

READING 1.1

Will Hutton: 'The State to Come'

Whether in trade, finance or the speed and scope of communication, the degree of interpenetration of national markets and cultures is unprecedented. We smoke Marlboro cigarettes, eat sushi, use [Microsoft] Windows ..., experiment with acupuncture, read *Cosmopolitan*, take away pizza and watch CNN wherever we are. English is emerging as the international language of communication whether it is for air-traffic control or scientific papers; the culture of the ski-resort, dealing room and airport is homogeneous. Blue jeans, sweatshirts and trainers are ubiquitous.

Source: Hutton, 1997, p.55

READING 1.2

Geoff Mulgan: 'The Age of Connexity'

For the vast majority of people, the basic fact of the modern world is that it is connected. Nowhere is remote in the way that so many places were remote a century, or even a generation, ago.

The simplest dimension of this connectedness is communication; today nearly a billion homes can talk to each other within a few seconds. Global positioning technologies can precisely track positions anywhere on the surface of the planet. Mobile phones can be carried up cliffs and into deserts. But there are other vital dimensions: global climate change, the decay of the ozone layer and the pollution of the oceans all bring the world's people closer together, if only because decisions made in one place shape other places. The result is an odd and novel situation. Remoteness and isolation were once the condition of the poor. Today it is only the super rich who can easily escape other people, and even they depend on armies of assistants to protect their privacy.

This degree of connectedness was not planned. No one had a blueprint for the shrinking of the world.

Source: Mulgan, 1998, p.19

READING 1.3

John Wiseman: 'Australia and the Politics of Globalisation'

Globalisation is the most slippery, dangerous and important buzzword of the late twentieth century. It is slippery because it can have many meanings and be used in many ways. It is dangerous because too often it is used as a powerful and simplistic justification for the endless expansion of unregulated capitalist relations into every part of life in every corner of the globe. It is important because debates about globalisation can illuminate a world in which time and space have been so dramatically compressed that distant actions in one corner of the globe have rapid and significant repercussions on people and places far away.

Source: Wiseman, 1998, p.1

READING 1.4

Anthony Giddens: 'Runaway World'

Although Giddens himself takes a rather different view, he neatly summarizes the views of those who see globalization as little more than Americanization:

'To many living outside Europe and North America [globalization]... looks like Westernisation – or, perhaps, Americanisation, since the US is now the sole superpower, with a dominant economic, cultural and military position in the global order. Many of the most visible cultural expressions of globalisation are American – Coca-Cola, McDonald's. ... [Since most multinational corporations are based in the US and the North,] a pessimistic view of globalisation would consider it largely an affair of the industrial North, in which the developing societies of the South play little or no active part. It would see it as destroying local cultures, widening world inequalities and worsening the lot of the impoverished. Globalisation, some argue, creates a world of winners and losers, a few on the fast track to prosperity, the majority condemned to a life of misery and despair ... [In the last decade of the twentieth century] the share of the poorest fifth of the world's population in global income has dropped from [an already miserable] 2.3 per cent to 1.4 per cent ... [while] some global corporations sell goods that are controlled or banned in the more prosperous countries of the North in less developed countries instead ... rather than "global village", this is more like "global pillage".'

Source: Giddens, 1999, Lecture 1

FIGURE 1.1   The impact of globalization? Watching television in an Indian village

COMMENT

The four readings clearly express different perceptions of globalization. The first stresses the extent to which globalization is characterized by the homogenization of economy and culture, the second looks at the significance of increased connectedness, the third highlights the extent to which globalization may be little more than the language of unregulated capitalism, while the fourth provides an interpretation of globalization that emphasizes the global power of America.

In some respects the readings offer what appear to be contradictory interpretations. So, for example, increasing global connectedness can seem threatening to our *local* world and Reading 1.1 could be read as supporting the *pessimistic* view that globalization is creating a society that is out of control. It suggests that globalizing forces are creating a more homogeneous society in a variety of ways, eroding cultural distinctions and imposing a 'global' economic and political system (a view also found in Readings 1.3 and 1.4). According to this way of interpreting social change, globalization is a threat to the histories and cultural differences in society, to traditional ways of life and to the scope for individual or collective agency or autonomy. It may mean that we have increasingly little choice about how our economies are run and how our jobs are organized – we have to accept pay cuts, new sorts of jobs or cuts in welfare spending, because if we do not, Britain (or any other country) will not be globally competitive.

A more *positive* view is also possible, however, perhaps reflected most clearly in Reading 1.2. In this case, living in a more global world is exciting as it opens up new opportunities and choices wherever we are. Local lives are lived in an increasingly *global* context. We can eat Thai food in a British city and get a taste of Australian life by turning on the TV set. Even the homogeneity identified in Reading 1.1 allows us to eat sushi and experiment with acupuncture.

As Mulgan has put it 'Much that was different is becoming standardised, but at the same time connexity makes it easier for bits of culture to be combined, hybridised and transformed' (Mulgan, 1998, p.22). Foreign travel can enrich our appreciation of other cultures while e-mail can keep us in touch across the world. Stretched social relations across space and growing interconnectedness across national boundaries allows us to reinterpret and refresh traditional local cultures and ways of life. So the free flow of goods, ideas, technologies and social practices across national borders may actually increase the scope for agency and eliminate negative aspects of national difference. It may also encourage (rather than discourage) the scope for local difference and diversity, since it is more difficult for nation-states to impose a uniform identity on their citizens, and connections between places often cut across national boundaries.

Reading 1.3 from John Wiseman indicates some of the major problems with the use of the term 'globalization', in that it is too readily used to explain any international phenomenon that is occurring. Moreover, it can be used to justify the activities of big corporations by superficially suggesting the inevitability of the process and assumed benefits from it. Wiseman is urging a more careful usage of the term, so that its actual character, extent and effects can be studied.

Reading 1.4 from Anthony Giddens provides a summary of one particular view, very different from his own, which identifies globalization with 'Americanization' and consequent detrimental effects on large sections of the world's population

---

The tensions identified in this section are fundamental to the debates about globalization developed in this chapter and in the later chapters of the book. How did you react to the issues raised by the readings? Do you see globalization positively or negatively? Are you simply sceptical about whether it is anything new? Are local lives and cultures threatened by global forces or are local histories re-framed in new and exciting ways by the presence of the global in the local? Perhaps your responses are uncertain or ambivalent, reflecting the complexity of the issues.

SUMMARY

Some preliminary conclusions can be drawn about what is meant by globalization.

- There are different views on what globalization means.
- It describes growing global interconnectedness.
- Some writers argue that it represents a significant shift in the spatial form of social relations so that the interaction between apparently local and global processes becomes increasingly important.
- It involves the organization and exercise of power on a global scale.
- It is a multi-dimensional process; it applies to the whole range of social relations – cultural, economic and political. Its effects can be seen in all aspects of social life from the food we eat and the TV we watch, to the sustainability of our environment.
- For some writers it can be seen positively and for others pessimistically. It may have benefits for society as well as risks. Local places and cultures can be seen as increasingly threatened by global flows or, alternatively, as reinvented through them in new and diverse ways.

3 DEFINING GLOBALIZATION: UNDERSTANDING GLOBAL CHANGE

3.1 Key concepts

There is a broad consensus among those that accept the notion of globalization that its most distinctive features or concepts can be summarized under four main headings.

3.1.1 Stretched social relations

It is argued that cultural, economic and political processes in society are increasingly **stretched** across nation-state boundaries so that events and decisions taking place on one side of the world have a significant impact on the other. Whereas **regionalization** can be defined as interconnectedness between 'geographically contiguous states' as in the case of Europe, one might reasonably expect globalization to involve transcontinental and inter-

Stretched social relations
The existence of cultural, economic and political networks of connection across the world.

Regionalization
Increased interconnection between states that border on each other.

regional relations that extend across the globe. Examples might be global climate change and environmental degradation (as in Mulgan, Reading 1.2) or unregulated capitalist relations (as in Wiseman, Reading 1.3). The stretching of social relations places us all within wider networks of connection to the extent that individual decisions may also have global consequences – some would argue, for example, that it is an accumulation of individual consumption decisions that has led to some of the global environmental problems we face today.

3.1.2 Intensification of flows

Intensification
Increased density of interaction across the globe which implies that the impacts of events are felt more strongly than before.

The stretching of social relations seems to be associated with an **intensification** of flows and networks of interaction and interconnectedness that transcend nation-states. One aspect of this is to be found in the density of communication and interaction. This point was illustrated in the Psion extract which stated that whereas in 1999 only 2 per cent of America was 'within four rings of the telephone ... soon instant communication will be available to all' (*The Guardian*, 20 March 1999). Although the US is still at the centre of these electronic flows, communications networks stretching across the world have the potential to connect people, previously distanced from what went on elsewhere, into a shared *social space* that is quite distinct from territorial space. So, for example, physical distance no longer works quite so effectively to dull the sensation when events such as famines, wars, terrorist attacks or massacres happen on the other side of the world. Instead of being separated from them, they are brought (albeit often in distorted – sometimes sanitized, sometimes sensationalized – form) into our living rooms.

3.1.3 Increasing interpenetration

Interpenetration
The extent to which apparently distant cultures and societies come face to face with each other at local level, creating increased diversity.

The increasing extent and intensity of global interactions is changing the geography of the relationship between the local and the global. As social relations stretch there is an increasing **interpenetration** of economic and social practices, bringing apparently distant cultures and societies face to face with each other at local level, as well as on the global stage. While Coca-Cola, McDonald's or Hollywood movies are obvious examples of the ways in which one culture's expressions (in this case the US's) are exported to other countries, the process works the other way too. As indicated in some of the readings, Western cultures increasingly reflect cultural influences from across the world. Mostafavi suggests that:

> Globalization can, in one sense, be viewed as reframing old colonial power relations, albeit without the necessity for actual physical occupation of territory – except that global cities such as London or New York are themselves now being colonised by people whose countries have been physically or economically colonised by the West.

(Mostafavi, 1999, p.9)

3.1.4 Global infrastructure

Interconnections that cross nation-state boundaries operate outside the systems of regulation and control of individual nations and are global not only in their operations but in their institutional **infrastructure**. On an institutional level, there are international organizations which supporters of the idea of a globalizing world would identify as the basic infrastructure for governing the global system. The United Nations organization and its various agencies have a role in the political and social sectors, passing resolutions on the activities of states such as Iraq and Israel, and providing assistance for health, refugees, education, cultural sites and so on. The World Bank and the International Monetary Fund are seen to provide the basis for regulating and stabilizing global finance, while the World Trade Organization is seen to regulate global trade. On a different level, information and communications technologies provide part of the infrastructure of interaction that supports the growth of global markets. According to this claim, nation-states find themselves at the mercy of these markets, which have powerful structural effects, severely limiting their policy options. We are seeing the emergence of a fundamental challenge to the sovereignty of the nation-state. Ohmae (1990) has suggested that we are moving into a 'borderless world' in which city regions or city states rather than nation-states will become the main basis of political organization. A few (world) cities become the nodes of global power, through which financial decision-making flows. Decisions taken in these citadels of power can have dramatic effects for the rest of us as stock markets wax and wane, chasing each other up and down the Nikkei, the NASDAQ, the FTSE and Dow Jones indices. For some, the key point is simply the existence of genuinely global ('free') markets, with rules that corporations, countries, people, labour and capital have to obey; while others would point to the emergence of transnational or global institutions of economic and political governance.

> **Infrastructure**
> The underlying formal and informal institutional arrangements that are required for globalized networks to operate.

3.2 Applying the concepts

How helpful are these characteristics in analysing what is actually going on – in understanding social change? How do they help us assess the impact of globalization on our everyday lives? To help us answer such questions, we will turn to a case study of the global transport of nuclear waste.

ACTIVITY 1.3

As you read the following case study, keep the concepts of 'stretching', 'intensity', 'interpenetration' and global 'infrastructure' in mind. Consider whether and in what ways the notion of globalization helps to develop our understanding of the processes at work in the transportation of nuclear waste.

BOX 1.1   **Case study – transporting nuclear waste**

In April 1986 an accident occurred at the Chernobyl nuclear power station in the USSR (a state that has since disappeared, which means that Chernobyl is now in the Ukraine). The effects of the blast were felt far from the local site of the accident. A cloud carrying radioactive particles across the north of Britain hit rainy weather and although it had been expected that the resulting fall-out would be short-term, ten years later 70,000 sheep in Cumbria remained contaminated. Within the former USSR it has been estimated that by the year 2040 there will have been over 16,000 deaths as a result of the radioactivity from Chernobyl.

Meanwhile, at Sellafield in Cumbria, the nuclear reactor and storage and reprocessing plant also represent a potentially significant environmental and social risk. Nuclear waste from all over Britain and even from Japan is taken to Sellafield for reprocessing. At the same time, Sellafield has produced plutonium for the British nuclear industry and for the US. Economic and political relations that link Britain with other nations across the globe are therefore inherent in the locally felt hazards of pollution in Cumbria.

The case of the privatized Aldermaston atomic weapons factory in the south of England demonstrates the potential local risks associated with the nuclear industry. When the Environment Agency inspected the plant in 1999, it found that contaminated water was being poured down surface drains without authorization. Large quantities of tritium-contaminated water were also found to be discharging into a brook flowing into a river that supplies drinking water to the town of Reading. Millions of pounds will have to be spent replacing pipe work at the plant that also threatens to poison Thames and London drinking water by contamination with even more dangerous plutonium particles (*Observer*, 21 February 1999).

Few communities are happy to have risks like these located close to them or near to their supply of drinking water, yet densely populated Britain has some of the world's largest stocks of radioactive waste. Local opposition has led to a political decision to abandon plans for a deep nuclear waste dump in Cumbria or anywhere else in Britain and to the search for an overseas dump. As an illustration of the complexity of networks of global connections and impacts, in 1999, the *Observer* reported on one plan which was said to have been financed by the British government-owned company, British Nuclear Fuels (BNFL). The plan was to ship the waste around the world to the 'doorstep' of an Aborigine community in Australia where it would remain radioactive for an estimated period of more than 250,000 years. The plan would be to build the world's biggest nuclear waste repository on Aboriginal land. A BNFL official, Bill Anderton, is reported as saying, 'We are a company involved in the forefront of nuclear technology and we are always seeking innovative solutions. Because of practical considerations, it's inevitable that there will be some degree of international collaboration in the construction of waste repositories. ... Australia has the right geology and the political stability vital for a deep disposal site. ... We believe there would be substantial economic and other benefits for Australia' (*Observer*, 21 February, 1999).

Meanwhile, local reactions in Australia were less enthusiastic. Aboriginal leaders referred to the destruction of ancient settlements and the local environment, including the threat to dozens of rare species. They said that Britain was 'treating them like dogs'. Aborigines were forced to leave their homeland nearly half a century earlier due to British atom bomb tests. One Aboriginal spokeswoman said, 'We have already suffered from mining and atomic bomb testing by Britain and others. We don't want our children killed by poison from Britain' (*Observer*, 21 February 1999).

FIGURE 1.2   Living with globalization; an Aboriginal youth in Australia

The logic of the global transportation of pollution was spelled out in the language of economics in a World Bank internal memorandum in 1991, written by Lawrence Summers, who was then chief economist at the World Bank. Summers identified three reasons for 'encouraging more migration of the dirty industries to the LDCs (Lesser-Developed Countries)'. The first was that the health costs of pollution in high wage countries was higher than in low wage countries, because it would be measured in terms of the income foregone by those who were ill or dying. The 'economic logic behind dumping a load of toxic waste in the lowest wage country,' he argued, 'is impeccable'. Second, he suggested that 'the under-populated countries of Africa are vastly *under*-polluted' since even a significant increase would be associated with only relatively small increases in terms of health and other consequences. Finally, he maintained that there was also likely to be more demand for a clean environment in countries with higher income levels. So, for example, he argued, an increased risk of prostate cancer as a result of pollution was more likely to be of concern to people in countries 'where people survive to get prostate cancer than in a country where under-5 mortality is 200 per thousand'. As a result he concluded that the export of pollution would be 'welfare enhancing', improving the position both for the exporters (in wealthy countries) who would benefit environmentally, and for the importers (in poor countries) who would benefit financially.

(quoted in Harvey 1995, p.65)

C O M M E N T

The case of the transportation of nuclear waste is clearly a complex one that can provoke strong feelings and reactions to the perceived uncertainties and risks associated with this form of pollution. Below we refer to each of the four key concepts of globalization to see what the notion tells us about the processes at work in this case study. As you read, think about whether or not those four concepts show that global change has altered so much that the world is now dramatically different from how it was before.

- The *stretching* of social relations across space is particularly clear. Decisions taken about nuclear power and its production in the one-time USSR had dramatic effects far away from the site of the Chernobyl plant. The reprocessing of nuclear waste is a global industry, and the search for places to dump nuclear waste is a global one, with a site in Australia apparently being particularly attractive for BNFL. The complexity of these relations and the world-wide focus of the search for a site is, at least, consistent with the globalization thesis. Although some might argue that Australia has been used in similar ways since the creation of the first British penal colony there, the new arrangements have less to do with British colonialism (or neo-colonialism) than the workings of an industry with a global reach. As the World Bank memo suggests, there is a new 'logic' which argues that flows of pollution from the richer countries of the North to the poorer countries of the South (the so-called 'lesser-developed countries') is a 'world welfare enhancing trade', because places with wide open spaces and little pollution are able to store the waste and will receive money for this service, so that their incomes are raised. This is a logic that builds on and reshapes existing patterns of uneven global development.

- The *intensity* of the interactions is apparent, too. An explosion in Chernobyl had a measurable effect thousands of miles away, as well as on the local environment. Local opposition to plans to dump nuclear waste in Cumbria could have a dramatic effect on the other side of the globe, where it is feared that children may be poisoned by the new pollution. Some might argue that Australian Aborigines faced similar threats when they were removed from the land to make way for the British nuclear tests in the 1950s, but this time the logic is driven by the requirements of global business rather than simple colonialism. In this context, it is also important to confirm that the impacts of globalizing processes are geographically uneven. While trade in waste is global, the impacts of pollution and the siting of waste dumps are local. In other words, the consequences of global decisions are felt more intensely in some places than in others, which may also reflect and reinforce unequal power relations.

- What about *interpenetration*? The impact of the Chernobyl incident on Britain and the potential impact of BNFL's investment decision on Australia are clear enough, but interpenetration would imply that there is also some sort of impact back. The case of Chernobyl certainly led to increased global concerns about the regulation of the nuclear industry, but – more importantly perhaps – it helped to confirm the Soviet Union's weaknesses as a technological superpower, playing a part – although not a determining one – in hastening the collapse of the existing state system. The role of Sellafield in Britain as a reprocessor of nuclear waste from Japan as well as Britain, the production of plutonium for the British and US nuclear industries, as well as the re-export of waste to other sites, suggests that a complex process of interaction is taking place through the global nuclear industry. And the way in which the local reactions to proposals to build the nuclear waste repository in Australia quickly ended up in the pages of newspapers (such as the *Observer*) back in the UK, suggests that there is a two-way process at work.

- The emergence of *global institutional infrastructures and networks* underpins much of the discussion around nuclear waste disposal, and is reinforced by the points made in Summers' memorandum. The World Bank certainly sees itself as having such a role as a key element in the global economic and trading infrastructure. However, it is important to note both that some of the transnational infrastructure is fairly rudimentary and that in the case of Chernobyl it was the inadequacy of any transnational regulatory agencies that helped to create the crisis. Some would argue that the key underpinning of globalization is simply the maintenance of a 'liberal' system of global trade, which ensures that the main economic players are allowed to move where and when they want without restriction.

SUMMARY

Applying the concepts associated with globalization to the nuclear waste case illustrates some of the key issues that inform theoretical debates about the nature and effects of global change. The significant points to emerge from the views that accept globalization are:

- globalization constitutes a shift in the geography of local and global social relations

- globalization is associated with unequal economic and power relations

- the effects of globalization are geographically uneven

- the four concepts of 'stretching', 'intensification', 'interpenetration' and 'infrastructure' are helpful in exploring the impact of globalization.

4 THE BIG DEBATES

In the next three chapters of this book you will be introduced to a range of different perspectives and evidence about global change in relation to the three areas of human activity – culture and communications, the economy and politics, which are explored in detail in Chapters 2 to 4. To help you assess the strengths and weaknesses of these perspectives, we will be using a theoretical framework that will help you to locate each perspective within three overarching approaches.

The three positions which sum up the debate on globalization may be termed the globalist, inter-nationalist, and transformationalist.

Globalists take the view that globalization is a real and tangible phenomenon. They argue that there has been a significant shift in the geography of social relations and that social processes now operate predominantly at a global scale. The impacts of globalization can be felt everywhere in the world and increasing global interconnections are making national boundaries less important. National cultures, economies and politics are subsumed into networks of global flows. These lessen local and national differences, autonomy and sovereignty, and produce a more homogeneous global culture and economy. Globalists point to the emergence of a new global structure whose rules determine how countries, organizations and people operate. According to this view, globalization is an inevitable trajectory of development, so any attempts to resist it are doomed to failure.

Optimists or *positive globalists* point to the benefits of globalization and see the results of globalizing influences as a change to be welcomed. They focus on the potential of stretched social relations to improve the quality of life, raise living standards and bring people together, which, in turn, promotes the sharing of cultures and understanding among nations around the world – in a sense making us all world citizens through global communication. While they recognize the dangers of global environmental pollution, positive globalizers argue that we could improve the position if we all took some responsibility for reducing unsustainable levels of consumption, and they point to the development of new technologies which are likely to reduce levels of pollution.

Pessimistic globalists, by contrast, see the world as becoming less diverse and more homogeneous. They emphasize the dominance of major economic and political interests – particularly in the countries of the North like the US, Western Europe and Japan – who are able effectively to resist all pressures for change, and can impose their own agenda on the world. They see the diminution of national identities and sovereignty negatively and point to the uneven consequences of globalization. They also focus on particular groups such as women and unskilled manual workers as major victims of globalization.

Globalists
They see globalization as an inevitable development which cannot be resisted or significantly influenced by human intervention, particularly through traditional political institutions, such as nation-states.

Conversely **inter-nationalists** are sceptical about globalization. They dispute the notion that there is evidence of a fundamental or systemic shift in social relations. They believe that globalization is a myth, or at any rate is much exaggerated as a distinctively new phenomenon, and emphasize continuities between the past and present. Inter-nationalists argue that in spite of increases in global flows of trade and money around the world, these are not substantially different from the economic and social interactions that have occurred between nations in previous historical times. The exchange of goods and cultures goes back to early times and in the nineteenth century, open trading and liberal economic relations were the norm world-wide. Globally powerful economic and political interests were not hard to find. What we are witnessing is, therefore, simply a continuation and progression of earlier world trading links. The more powerful states still have the freedom to act in their own interests as they did in the past. Inter-nationalists see the majority of economic and social activity as still being essentially regional rather than truly global in spatial scale – the European Union would be cited as an example of the increased importance of regionalization, rather than globalization.

In the search for solutions, inter-nationalists emphasize that nation-states retain much more room for manoeuvre than the globalists are ready to admit. They believe that there is still significant scope for nations (as relatively autonomous agencies) to determine their own economic and political priorities and to defend post-Second World War welfare states. The dismissal of such policies by the globalists is, in turn, dismissed as little more than an ideological crusade by big business reluctant to pay taxes or pay adequate wages. Inter-nationalists support the resistance of groups to the development priorities of global business and seek to challenge the global inequalities produced by those priorities. Like pessimistic globalists inter-nationalists have raised the concerns of women and unskilled workers affected by the activities of global business and the more powerful states.

A third – **transformationalist** – approach agrees with the inter-nationalists that the globalists have exaggerated their case. They argue that nation-states remain militarily, economically and politically powerful. However, while some scepticism is justified, they also believe that it is foolhardy to dismiss the notion of globalization or underestimate its material impacts and effects.

According to this view, the consequences of contemporary global interactions are complex, diverse and unpredictable; further, their effects are uneven and warrant serious study and concern. In other words, while the form of global social relations may not display a significant shift, the characteristics are distinctive. The autonomy of nation-states is constrained by forms of transnational power that are not accountable either because they reflect the priorities of major corporations pursuing their own commercially driven goals, or because of the overriding need to compete effectively in global markets. In consequence it is not that globalists are inherently wrong but that globalization should not be understood as an inevitable or a fixed end point. Rather, it

Inter-nationalists
They argue that the significance of globalization as a new phase has been exaggerated. They believe that most economic and social activity is regional, rather than global, and still see a significant role for nation-states.

Transformationalists
They believe that globalization represents a significant shift, but question the inevitability of its impacts. They argue that there is still significant scope for national, local and other agencies.

should be conceived as a complex set of interconnecting relationships through which power, for the most part, is exercised indirectly.

Transformationalists argue that the precise forms taken by globalization are not inevitable and may be reversible. Solutions are likely to be based on new and progressive structures for democratic accountability and a global system of governance. In this system, global institutions would be democratized and empowered but nation-states retain a key role as territorially specific, legitimate and accountable frameworks for policy. Transformationalists emphasize the importance of interaction between the structural context represented by globalizing tendencies and initiatives taken by national, local and other agencies in defining what is possible.

ACTIVITY 1.4

As you work through this book you will develop a fuller understanding of these different theoretical approaches. To help you reflect on the issues we have covered so far, consider what the three approaches would have to say about global change in the case of nuclear waste (Section 3.2). Keep a note of your thoughts on the three approaches in the table below. Which of them do you think is most helpful in the context of the case study?

TABLE 1.1   Theoretical approaches to globalization: the case of nuclear waste

Theoretical approach	
Globalist (positive)	Benfits both coutries enivitable, "logical"
Globalist (pessimistic)	forcing negative aspects onto others Destroying contine, Domination
Inter-nationalist	Nothing changed
Transformationalist	Possible to prevent

COMMENT

For globalists the message of the case study on nuclear waste is that it is necessary to learn to live with the new global regime – the extract quoted from the World Bank memorandum which stresses the value of the trade in pollution is consistent with a globalist view. Summers, himself, would probably be seen as an optimist, but it would be equally possible to view this outcome pessimistically, from the perspective of someone who was unpersuaded by his argument. Inter-nationalists might argue that nothing much has really changed. The relationship is simply an extension of old colonial relationships and global inequality is nothing new. Transformationalists would argue that there are significant shifts in the relationships – this really is a global trade, rather than one that reflects colonial relationships – but suggest that there are opportunities for both the Aborigines and the Australian government to question the proposal and resist the implications of having a global market in pollution.

5 LOOKING FOR THE EVIDENCE

Before we can go on to evaluate the different perspectives on global change that are developed in the chapters that follow, we need to consider what sort of quantitative and qualitative evidence might help us to assess whether globalization is a significant phenomenon or just a political and academic fad, and whether it really is having a significant impact on economic and social relations. Exploring the evidence for globalization is difficult and controversial but it is a necessary step to take. In this section we consider just some of the different forms of evidence that need to be assessed. Here we return to the features we identified in Section 3 to consider some possible indicators that should help us judge whether globalization is taking place, and, if so, how it is constituted.

Have social and economic relations stretched across space?

Some examples might include:

● Looking at flows of migration across boundaries and the survival of significant linkages and networks between members of (one-time) migrant populations who find themselves in a range of different countries. The existence, sustenance and development of shared cultural forms that cross national boundaries (sometimes referred to as 'diaspora cultures') suggest a stretching of social relations between people across space. Examples might include the linkages among Chinese communities outside China (Allen, 1999, pp.212–4) or the complex linkages among black people through what Gilroy (1993) calls the 'black Atlantic'. Of course, sceptics might point to the historical significance of the Jewish diaspora and question whether we are really seeing anything that is new.

- It is important to assess whether flows of trade and investment stretch across the globe or remain restricted to relatively small parts of it. If most economic exchange is restricted to a relatively small number of countries, then it is legitimate to question some of the grander claims of globalization (see Chapter 3). In the debate between globalists and inter-nationalists, it is important to identify whether (and in what ways) patterns of trade have changed since the nineteenth century.

- In what ways does the environmental pollution produced by the wealthy nations of the North have effects that stretch out, potentially threatening global environmental sustainability? Mapping some of the flows and interconnections between places would help to show the extent to which globalization is taking place beyond nation-states, across political boundaries and beyond regions.

Have increased intensification of flows crossed the globe?

Examples might include:

- The spread of communications technologies to most countries of the world. This is relatively easy to track and is reflected in the battle for global supremacy between the small British company Psion and the Microsoft 'monolith' that was discussed in Section 2. It is important to clarify the extent to which these technologies are actively used in different societies and by what proportion of the population. So in the debate between globalists and traditionalists, it is important to clarify whether there has merely been a change of scale or if there has been a change that transforms the ways in which we live our lives.

- Looking back over a relatively short period (five to ten years), we may be able to assess the rate at which change is taking place. For example you could look at the rate at which mobile telephone use or access to satellite television is increasing, or even the density of American fast food outlets as they spread across the globe.

- The extent to which global cultural phenomena cross the world and the density of their coverage. Is there evidence that instantaneous communication means we feel closer to some global icons (such as Nelson Mandela) than we do to our next door neighbour? How much influence does Hollywood have on our daily lives (see Chapter 2)? Similarly, is the Indian cinema industry ('Bollywood') becoming a feature of global cultural life?

FIGURE 1.3   Cultural interpenetration: a Bollywood film hoarding, Bombay, 2002

- The volume of trade and level of exchange between countries and across continents and the amount by which they have increased. This provides an important source of evidence of the intensification of economic flows.

- The increase and globalization of migration across nation-state political boundaries, with more countries being affected and a growth in the volume of migration in all regions of the world (Castles and Miller, 1993). The challenge is to assess whether responses to this phenomenon can be handled through traditional (nation-state based) arrangements or whether new forms of global governance are required.

- Is the presence or absence of foreign investment dominating the political economic development of large areas of the world?

Is there extensive interpenetration of economic and social practices?

Examples might include:

- The extent to which US cultural forms have been exported to other countries. This can be measured relatively straightforwardly but, additionally, it is important to assess the ways these exports are reinterpreted and reworked in the importing countries. Evidence of interpenetration should highlight the ways in which there has been a reverse export or a complex pattern of exchange and learning, for example the incorporation of new ways of thinking and new cultural forms and identities (**Woodward, 2004**).

FIGURE 1.4   Buying fast food in Indonesia

Finding evidence of these cultural forms of interpenetration represents a bigger challenge than counting the flows of imports and exports. Examples might include the popularity of Brazilian soap operas on Portuguese television or the way in which 'Indian' food is increasingly marketed to tourists coming to Britain as typically 'British'.

- Zukin (1995), in her discussion of restaurants in New York, argues that the extensive involvement of immigrants in different aspects of the restaurant trade (albeit particularly at the low paid, casualized end of the labour market) encourages the bringing together of the 'global and local markets of both employees and clientele' (p.158). Restaurants, she says, produce an increasingly global product tailored to local tastes (p.182).

- The local juxtaposition of diverse cultures and different traditions – although a traditionalist might ask whether there is much new about the existence of ghettos and social divisions along racial or cultural lines in cities. However the scale and complexity may be different. Davis (1993, p.41) suggests that the 'neighbourhood geography of Los Angeles has redrawn the map of the world to place El Salvador next to Korea, Armenia next to Thailand, Samoa next to Belize, and Louisiana next to Jalisco'.

- The export of goods and services or patterns of foreign direct investment in different countries (such as levels of Japanese, British or German investment in the US). This highlights the extent to which movement is largely one way, as well as indicating how much of the globe is actually involved in the process.

Is there the emergence of a global infrastructure?

Examples might include:

- The growth of information and communications technologies as a global system. Perhaps the most obvious example is the development of the Internet, whose global reach could be explored and assessed. Others include the spread of satellite-based systems both for television broadcasts and for other forms of communication, including mobile telephone networks.

- The emergence and growth of increasingly sophisticated global financial markets, particularly as there is now effectively 24 hour trading across the world between the big exchanges in London, New York and Tokyo. Even in the financial sector, however, it is important to explore the extent to which national differences still matter, as well as the extent to which smaller exchanges survive (and prosper) in a range of countries. Variation between banking systems might undermine the arguments of the more enthusiastic globalists.

- The experience of particular countries that have attempted to resist the pressures of the global market, for example in refusing to devalue currencies or in sustaining welfare expenditure. Their success or failure would be an indicator of the extent of their continued sovereign agency.

- The growth of new forms of global governance through a proliferation of transnational interconnections between national governments, institutions and non-governmental organizations. This might indicate a reduced role for nation-states, at least unless they form alliances with others. The formal governance associated with nation-states relates to specific geographical boundaries and is, therefore, spatially confined. Debates about genetically modified food and the trade in bananas are handled through global organizations such as the World Trade Organization. These are sometimes seen simply as being dominated by big companies or particular countries but, in practice, they may have more autonomy than this suggests. The European Union is another example of such an organization, creating a regional partnership within a globalizing world. McGrew (1995) identifies a wide range of cross-national institutions and networks, for example in the fields of security (e.g. NATO), telecommunications and human rights. One means of measuring this would be to chart the increase in international governmental organizations (which might include the EU, NATO, the UN, the World Trade Organization among others) and non-governmental organizations (such as Greenpeace, Oxfam, and the Catholic Church). Chapter 4 of this book discusses the growth of such organizations.

● It might be argued that the role of NATO in the bombing of Serbia in 1999 was no more than that of an alliance between sovereign nations, but the way in which the countries acted together suggests that NATO is more of a global – or transgovernmental – organization. Certainly, from a Serb perspective, although Kosovo is a province of Yugoslavia, it is pretty clear that the presence of internationally recognized borders was not perceived as giving the Yugoslav government a monopoly on the means of violence within those borders. Events taking place within the borders of one state became matters of wider global concern, leading to external intervention.

SUMMARY

The globalist, inter-nationalist and transformationalist positions on globalization all support their arguments by selecting different forms of evidence and by interpreting specific pieces of evidence in different ways. While indicators, for example, of the number of transnational corporations and their share of global markets, the size of migrant populations or ecological footprints, provide vital clues to the extent and intensity of some flows and interconnections, other criteria, such as the degree of cultural transmission or social inequality, cannot be measured so easily.

6 MAPPING GLOBALIZATION

Globalization is a term which attempts to address complex phenomena and capturing its meaning in words is not always easy. One way of taking things further might be to explore its meaning through maps, particularly since most of us will be familiar with some of the ways in which the world has been depicted in atlases and on globes.

It is easy to take maps for granted – road maps help to guide us between towns and cities; street maps help us to find places we want to get to; we might use Ordnance Survey maps to guide us when we go for walks in the countryside. Few of us can probably remember a time in our lives when we didn't understand how to use maps like these, at least at a basic level.

And yet maps are actually quite complicated abstractions. They are not simple photographs of reality, but representations of reality which those preparing them (and reading them) wish to emphasize. They are highly selective in what information is included or excluded. So, for example, a street map of a town or city will rarely identify topography, whereas we might want that sort of information if we plan to go walking in the countryside. Each map, it appears, is designed according to the job it is expected to perform. But maps also reflect (and may reinforce) particular ways of understanding the world. As Doreen Massey puts it: '*maps are means of representation* and every individual map embodies a particular understanding, a particular interpretation, of the place it is depicting' (Massey, 1995, p.20, emphasis in the original).

The different positions on the question of globalization – the globalist, the inter-nationalist and the transformationalist – all envisage the world in different ways. Each position will pick out certain features of global relationships and see others as less important. To understand how different views on globalization could be expressed in different visual representations, let's start a couple of steps back.

The importance of maps as forms of representation is particularly clear when you look at the attempts that have been made to map the globe. There is, of course, a fundamental problem in attempting to do this in two dimensions on a sheet of paper since the world is three-dimensional – something close to spherical. But there is a bigger issue here relating to the ways in which the translation from three to two dimensions is made.

For a long time the most popular cartographic representation of the world was the one produced by the Mercator projection (see Figure 1.5 overleaf).

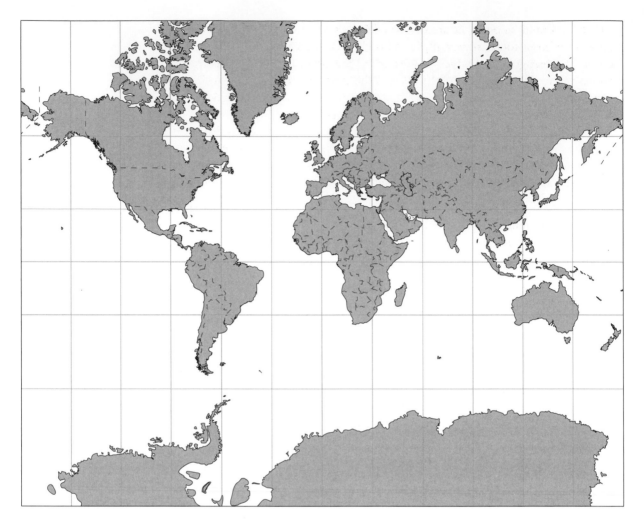

FIGURE 1.5   The world according to Mercator

It was initially created to assist European traders in navigation and it has the advantage of fairly accurately delineating the shapes of the various continents. Yet, in one very important sense, the map produced is highly misleading. It implies that the countries of the northern hemisphere are much larger in area relative to those of the southern hemisphere than they actually are. It is perhaps not surprising, therefore, that the Mercator projection's high point as the 'standard classroom wall-map' (Wright, 1993, p.38) coincided with the period in which European (and US) dominance, particularly colonial dominance, was taken for granted. Until the 1960s, in British schools at least, the colour pink was imposed on the map to highlight the UK's imperial (and later Commonwealth) reach.

The world according to Mercator makes the UK look larger than it is, compared to its colonial possessions. In addition, the importance of the UK is emphasized as the map is focused on the Greenwich meridian, so the

UK is presented as being at the centre of the globe. A map that chooses to have a different focus, for example the middle of the Pacific, gives quite a different message about which countries are important and which less so. Similarly the dominant model that places the northern hemisphere at the top of maps (because that is where we all 'know' the 'North' is) also makes it difficult to escape from the understanding that the North is the most powerful and the most important part of the globe. It is perhaps only when you see the map inverted, for example, with Australia at the top (as in Figure 1.6 overleaf), that you start to realize how much our view of the world is actually shaped by cartographic representations.

One way of seeing how a different map projection can produce different messages and reflect different understandings of the world is to look at the world as represented through the Peters projection (Figure 1.7 overleaf).

In this projection (more accurately, but less popularly, known as the Gall equal area projection) the emphasis is on ensuring that the relative areas of the different continents are accurately expressed (it is an 'equal area' map). In area, at least, the UK and Europe now take on a rather more modest global role, reflecting the understanding that other parts of the world are equally, if not more, important. The map itself has its own weaknesses, for example it significantly distorts the shapes of the continents. Other attempts have been made to compromise between the two models (Wright, 1993, p.45) but each of these, of course, makes its own representational compromises (and has its own meaning).

The most familiar maps of the world emphasize the borders within it – they identify countries and the boundaries between them. In the past, they emphasized the colonial possessions of the European powers as they stretched across the globe. In recent decades, however, keeping up with the changes has been a real challenge to the map-makers. At the start of the 1990s, no sooner had the USSR broken up into its component nations and new atlases been issued to reflect this, than Yugoslavia started to go through its painful reshaping. Figure 1.8 (overleaf) shows the changes of sovereignty that have taken place since 1939. It is remarkable how few parts of the world have been unaffected by these changes. But it is also important to recognize that, however significant the process of globalization, boundaries are still important means by which states identify the areas over which they have jurisdiction. It is perhaps also worth noting that there has been a dramatic growth in the number of nation-states since 1945, and even since the 1980s.

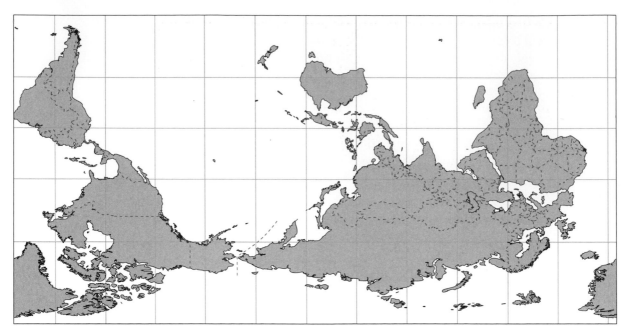

FIGURE 1.6   Australia at the top of the world

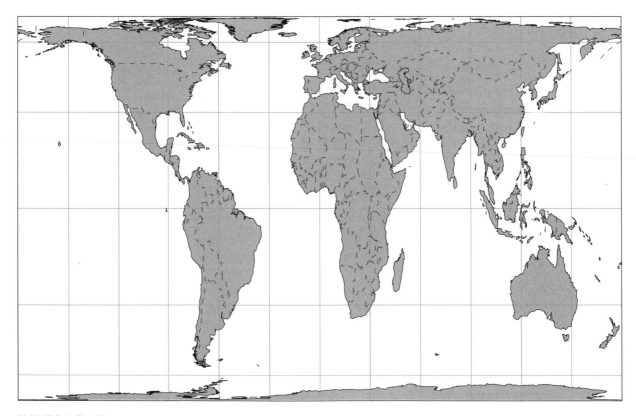

FIGURE 1.7   The world according to Peters

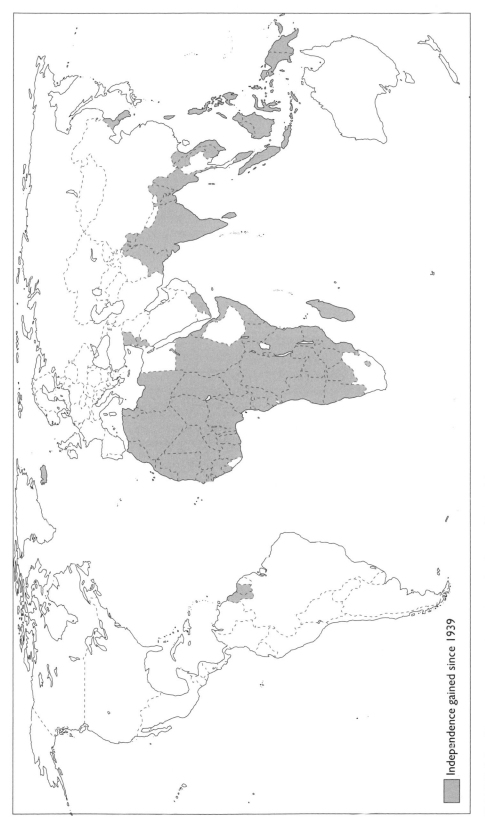

FIGURE 1.8   Changes in sovereignty since the Second World War

Independence gained since 1939

Not all representations of the world present it with borders, however. The picture of a spinning blue globe with partial cloud cover, as shown in Figure 1.9, has become a familiar image since the advent of space flight.

FIGURE 1.9   'Spaceship Earth'

In one sense we could simply say that this is a straightforward picture of 'reality' – after all it is a photograph. But in practice we might want to ask some questions. What message does such a picture give us? This is a powerful representation; it shows the world as a single entity rather than a space divided by political boundaries. It suggests to us that there is 'one world', that we are all passengers on 'Spaceship Earth', that we have the same broadly shared experience. Is this a more accurate representation of the world in which we live than the one that emphasizes boundaries and divisions?

In some respects, Figure 1.10 (opposite) is recognizable as a world map on which we can see the familiar shapes of some countries and some

FIGURE 1.10   World map showing GDP in a range of countries (1997)

Source: *Financial Times*, 27 November. 1999; from data provided by CIA Directorate of Intelligence; based on 1997 GDP, in purchasing-power parity terms. Not all countries are shown and many are not represented

continents. But it also presents a view of the world that indicates that the divisions that still exist between passengers on 'Spaceship Earth'. The relative size of the countries is an expression of the national income (gross domestic product) of each of them at the end of the twentieth century. On this map, the bigger the country, the bigger the national income. It is unlikely to change much in the twenty-first century. The divide between a relatively prosperous 'North' (including Australia and New Zealand) and a poor 'South' should be apparent (despite some significant differences within the North and the South). This map highlights some of the unevenness (and inequalities) of the world.

According to Castells (1998, pp.70–165), however, unevenness and inequality is not just apparent on this scale. Globalization, he argues, creates unexpected linkages through patterns of migration and creates a global elite with a similar lifestyle in every big city of the world. At the same time, he says, it generates a pool of migrant and local labour that exists at the bottom of the labour market in every world city. He uses the notion of the 'Fourth World' to identify those who are excluded from the economic flows associated with globalization. Those who are disconnected are effectively excluded from participation in the new global economy. The 'Fourth World' is, he says, 'made up of multiple black holes of social exclusion throughout the planet'. The 'Fourth World', he argues, is 'present in literally every country, and every city, in this new geography of social exclusion. It is formed of American inner-city ghettos, Spanish enclaves of mass youth unemployment, French *banlieues* warehousing North Africans, Japanese Yoseba quarters and Asian mega-cities' shanty towns. And it is populated by millions of homeless, incarcerated, prostituted, criminalised, brutalised, stigmatised, sick, and illiterate persons' (Castells, 1998, pp.164–5). Capturing all this on a map might encourage us to view the new world rather differently.

The ways in which we map the globe tell us about the ways in which we understand it. But how can maps be used to capture the complexity, the flows and interconnections as well as the breaks and disjunctions that some writers regard as features of globalization? Is there any way in which the relationships associated with globalization can be explicitly represented in maps?

One fairly straightforward way of mapping the global is to identify flows between key nodes across the world. So, for example, it is possible to identify world cities and mark the connections between them, as shown in Figure 1.11.

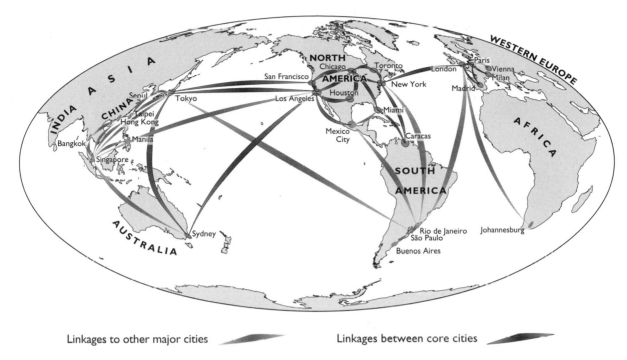

Linkages to other major cities   Linkages between core cities

FIGURE 1.11   Connecting world cities

Another might be to map the international production system of just one major multinational, as Figure 1.12 overleaf does for Volkswagen. Just presenting the information like this can make us view the world in a different way – it encourages us to think about sets of relationships that stretch across the globe and to question an approach dominated by national politics, national economies and national boundaries.

Another approach is to re-imagine the world in terms of time and space rather than the traditional notions of distance. For example, it is possible to produce a map that shows the relationship between places in terms of the travel time between them, rather than in miles or kilometres. Figure 1.13 shows a familiar picture of the Pacific, while Figure 1.14 reconfigures the same area along different lines. The distances in Figure 1.14 are based not on physical distance but on the times it takes to travel between places by scheduled airlines. The picture is now quite different, with some places brought closer together while others are forced apart, and places with little or no contact with scheduled airlines are effectively forced off the map altogether. The fluidity of the process is reinforced once you realize that the mapping in Figure 1.14 is based on scheduled flights in 1975. The picture would be different today, but some places are still outside the charmed circle of air travel.

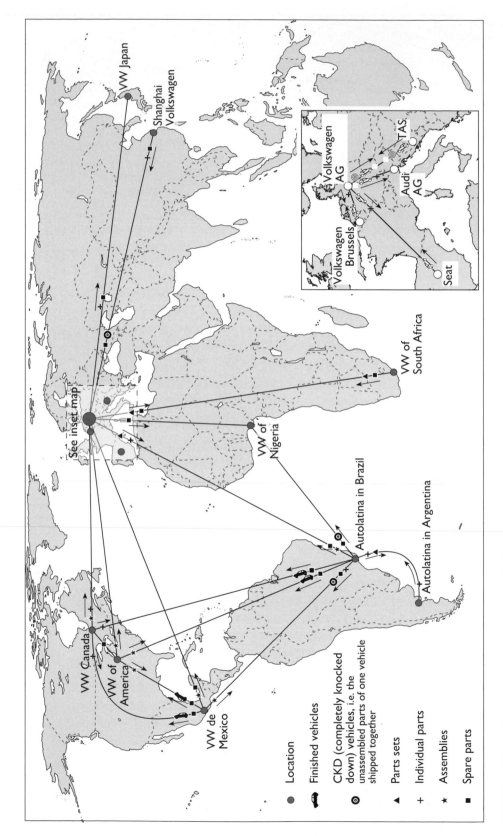

FIGURE 1.12 Volkswagen's international production system

Source: Knox and Agnew, 1998

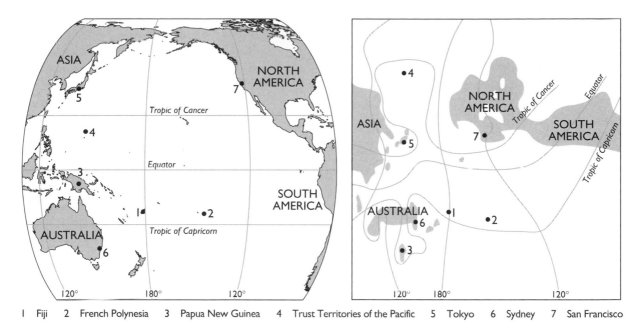

| 1 | Fiji | 2 | French Polynesia | 3 | Papua New Guinea | 4 | Trust Territories of the Pacific | 5 | Tokyo | 6 | Sydney | 7 | San Francisco |

FIGURE 1.13   Conventional projection of the Pacific in terms of distances

FIGURE 1.14   Time–space map of the Pacific, based on relative time accessibility by scheduled airline in 1975

Source: adapted from Haggett, 1990, Figure 3.3(c)

A C T I V I T Y   1 . 5

Thinking back to the example of the transportation of nuclear waste in Section 3.2, what kinds of maps might help our understanding of the process of global change in this case?

C O M M E N T

As we saw in Section 3.2, understanding the processes involved in the transportation of nuclear waste is far from straightforward. It would be necessary to illustrate a range of cultural, economic and political flows that cross the globe, not just between Britain and Australia, but also between these countries and the rest of the world through overlaying networks of interconnections. Think back to Summers' explanation of the logic behind the global transport of pollution. This suggests that in order to understand the processes involved, we also need to find a way to represent the underlying differences in standards of living, health and environments, as well as consumption and pollution, that are associated with uneven patterns of global development.

Clearly, maps can be very powerful tools to help us understand (or misunderstand) the processes of globalization and social change but capturing the full complexity and consequences of global change as it affects us in our daily lives is difficult. In a series of pictures titled *Small Worlds*, the artist Wassily Kandinsky sought to do just this in the 1920s. By identifying the boundaries within which we live and highlighting the networks of social relations that stretch across those boundaries, the pictures capture the stability and the fragility of social relations in an age of globalization. One of Kandinsky's drawings is reproduced as Figure 1.15. Maybe it is not strictly a 'map' (we're not sure quite what the different symbols represent!) but it should inspire us to think about the challenge of trying to summarize the complexity, speed, excitement and impact of the interactions associated by some writers with globalization.

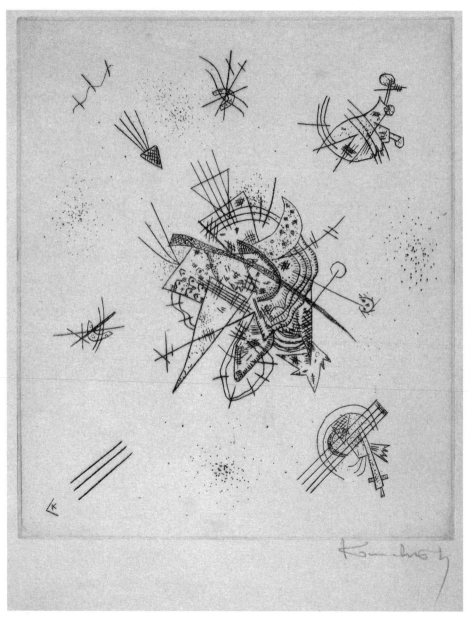

FIGURE 1.15   *Small Worlds X*, Kandinsky, 1922
© ADAGP, Paris and DACS, London 2000

SUMMARY

Studying the potential of maps to help our understanding of how different interpretations of the world can be expressed in different representations, suggests that:

- maps of the world have always presented particular understandings and interpretations

- the globalist, inter-nationalist and transformationalist views could be expressed in representations of the world and relationships within it

- the different views would highlight their own understandings of connections and disconnections associated with cross-national social flows and networks, the relevance or irrelevance of territorial state boundaries, and economic and power relations across and between states.

7 CONCLUSION

We have come a long way from the relatively simple story of globalization that was set out at the beginning of the chapter. As we have seen, globalization is a contested and controversial subject. There does seem to be broad agreement that something is happening, but rather less agreement about precisely what it is. In the chapter we have, therefore, set out to introduce you to the main features by which the debates over globalization may be characterized. In seeking to define whether globalization can be said to have occurred, we have stressed the importance of:

- the stretching of social and economic relations

- the intensification of communication and other linkages

- the interpenetration of economic and social practices

- the emergence of global infrastructure.

If globalization is taking place then we would expect these features to be present, and in the last two sections of the chapter we explored some of the ways in which we might look for evidence of their existence.

Equally important, however, we have introduced the main lines of debate that take place around the notion of globalization. We have characterized the main lines of argument around three positions – those of the globalists, the inter-nationalists and the transformationalists. The globalists are convinced that globalization is taking place and dramatically changing the social and economic context. The inter-nationalists are rather more sceptical. While they may acknowledge that change is taking place, they question the extent to which we are seeing a systemic shift. Instead they emphasize continuity with the past. Transformationalists recognize the strength of the inter-nationalists' challenge but believe they are underestimating the scale of change taking place and its significance. They believe that a major transformation is taking place, but do not accept (as globalists tend to) that outcomes are pre-determined. Instead, they argue that there is room for action by traditional agencies (such as nation-states) as well as the need to develop new approaches. These three approaches form the basis of the argument in the rest of the book.

REFERENCES

Allen, J. (1999) 'Cities of power and influence: settled formations' in Allen, J., Massey, D. and Pryke, M. (eds) *Unsettling Cities. Movement/Settlement*, London, Routledge, pp.181–227.

Allen, J. (2004) 'Power: its institutional guises (and disguises)' in Hughes, G. and Fergusson, R. (eds) *Ordering Lives: Family, Work and Welfare* (2nd edn), London, Routledge/The Open University.

Arlidge, J. (1999) *The Observer*, 21 February.

Castells, M. (1998) *End of Millennium*, Volume 3 of *The Information Age: Economy, Society and Culture*, Oxford, Blackwell.

Castles, S. and Miller, M.J. (1993) *The Age of Migration: International Population Movements in the Modern World*, New York, The Guilford Press.

Davis, M. (1993) 'Who killed Los Angeles? Part Two: the verdict is given', *New Left Review*, 199, pp.29–54.

Financial Times (1999) 'Buying powers', 27 November 1999.

Giddens, A. (1999) *Runaway World, The BBC Reith Lectures*, London, BBC Radio 4, BBC Education.

Gilroy, P. (1993) *The Black Atlantic: Modernity and Double Consciousness*, London, Verso.

Haggett, P. (1990) *The Geographer's Art*, Oxford, Basil Blackwell.

Harvey, D. (1995) 'The environment of justice' in Merrifield, A. and Swyngedouw, E. (1996) *The Urbanisation of Injustice*, London, Lawrence and Wishart.

Held, D. (1995) *Democracy and the Global Order: From the Modern State to Cosmopolitan Governance*, Cambridge, Polity.

Hutton, W. (1997) *The State to Come*, London, Vintage.

Knox, P. and Agnew, J. (1998) *The Geography of the World Economy*, London, Arnold.

McGrew, A. (1995) 'World order and political space' in Anderson, J., Brook, C. and Cochrane, A. (eds) *A Global World? Re-ordering Political Space*, Oxford, Oxford University Press.

Massey, D. (1995) 'Imagining the world' in Allen, J. and Massey, D. (eds) *Geographical Worlds*, Oxford, Oxford University Press.

Mostafavi, M. (1999) in Bradley, F. (ed.) *Cities on the Move, Urban Chaos and Global Change, East Asian Art, Architecture and Film Now*, London, Hayward Gallery, pp.7–9.

Mulgan, G. (1998*) Connexity: Responsibility, Freedom, Business and Power in the New Century,* London, Vintage.

Ohmae, K. (1990) *The Borderless World: Power and Strategy in the Interlinked Economy*, London, Collins.

Wiseman, J. (1998) *Global Nation? Australia and the Politics of Globalisation*, Cambridge, Cambridge University Press.

Woodward, K. (2004) 'Questions of identity' in Woodward, K. (ed.) *Questioning Identity: Gender, Class, Ethnicity* (2nd edn), London, Routledge/The Open University.

Whitford, F. (1999) *Kandinsky: Watercolours and Other Works on Paper,* London, Royal Academy of Art.

Wright, D. (1993) 'Maps with a message', *Geographical*, vol.LXV, no.1, pp.37–41.

Zukin, S. (1995) *The Cultures of Cities*, Oxford, Blackwell.

FURTHER READING

There is a very extensive literature on globalization, so any selection we make can only scratch the surface. We have chosen three books that provide rather different ways into the debate.

Hirst, P. and Thompson, G. (1999) *Globalization in Question: The International Economy and the Possibilities of Governance* (2nd edn) Cambridge, Polity.

Hirst and Thompson challenge some of the bigger claims made for economic globalization on the basis of a careful review of the available evidence. They suggest that there is still scope for nation-states to develop their own economic policies and highlight the scope for international collaboration, which does not undermine national autonomy. This is a creative book that builds on what we have called an inter-nationalist approach.

Mulgan, G. (1998) *Connexity: Responsibility, Freedom, Business and Power in the New Century*, London, Vintage.

This is a committed enthusiast's view of globalization. It is an entertaining – if rather polemical – read. Mulgan is an optimistic globalist who believes that we have to find ways of adjusting our lifestyles and business practices to fit in with its priorities.

Wiseman, J. (1998) *Global Nation? Australia and the Politics of Globalisation*, Cambridge, Cambridge University Press.

Wiseman takes a fairly sceptical approach to globalization, but argues that it represents a significant change in the way the world is organized. Because he comes at the debate through the case of Australia, the book challenges the way in which Europeans tend to think about the process. In terms of the model introduced in the chapter, he could be described as a transformationalist.

The globalization of culture?

Hugh Mackay

Contents

1 INTRODUCTION

Globalization is about the growing worldwide interconnections between societies, as we saw in Chapter 1. Culture – the focus of this chapter – is in many senses the most direct, obvious and visible way in which we experience these interconnections in our daily lives. It is a crucial component of globalization because it's through culture that common understandings are developed, so culture is central to connections between places and nations. Across the breadth of everyday activities there is a considerable body of evidence to suggest that our cultural traits, practices and goods – the assemblage we use to construct meaning symbolically – are increasingly global. Indeed, whatever globalization has been achieved – to the extent that it has – can be seen as a result of the growing significance of the symbolic, of the power of the cultural.

Although the globalization of culture seems in some ways obvious in our daily lives, it is not an entirely straightforward matter. Culture is a complicated and pervasive phenomenon, taking many forms. This chapter focuses on the media and, in particular, the popular cultural form of television. In the contemporary era, culture has become increasingly mediated; and television-viewing is a major leisure activity in the Western world. The chapter explores the various positions in the globalization debate which have been outlined in Chapter 1. It starts, in Section 2, with the arguments of those who see the decline of national cultures and the rise to the fore of global culture flows. Broadly speaking, these *globalists* fall into two categories. On the one hand are those who see the phenomenon in a *positive* way – such as those who argue that, with new communication technologies, we are moving towards a 'global village' in which communication and community can be freed from their physical or geographical constraints and a greater diversity of voices can be heard. On the other hand are the *pessimists* who, focusing on structures, point to the profound and growing inequalities which characterize patterns of ownership of information and communication devices, infrastructure and flows. They point also to the homogenizing consequences of global communication networks and cultural flows. This notion – that cultures around the world are becoming more homogeneous – is a key component of the **cultural imperialism** thesis, which is perhaps the longest-standing and best developed approach to explaining cultural globalization. It focuses on *structured patternings* of global domination and is a perspective we shall explore in some detail.

Cultural imperialism
Cultural goods flow to the rest of the world, inculcating US or Western values in those in recipient nations. This process prepares the ground for the import of other Western goods.

Next, in Section 3, we shall examine briefly the other side, the arguments of the *inter-nationalists*, those who are sceptical about processes of globalization. As we shall see, the media and other areas of cultural production remain stubbornly local and national in their organization, content and audiences, despite the powerful forces of globalization. We shall consider some important ways in which the media are best understood as national rather than global phenomena; and as best characterized in terms of continuity rather than revolution. We shall see that past eras have experienced dramatically and perhaps more forcefully than us today the impact of new communication technologies.

In Section 4 we shall explore the perspectives of *transformationalists*: those who see important changes in global flows taking place, but who point to the diverse and unpredictable consequences of the globalization of culture. In particular, we shall look at the complexities of cultural flows. The reality is that these are not simply one-way, from the Western world to the developing world, but are more fragmented and diverse. As well as flows, we shall examine some *qualitative* evidence about the significance and diversity of the local consumption of global culture; this informs us about the *impact* of the global flows which are taking place. In doing this we shall be focusing on consumers – not as passive recipients of structured inequalities, but as creative *agents* who actively make meanings as they consume cultural products.

2 GLOBALISTS

2.1 The global flows of culture

We can be quite clear that, in recent decades, there has been a phenomenal growth in the global circulation – in terms of both distance and volume – of cultural goods. This will probably come as no surprise to you if you think about what you watch on television and at the cinema. It exemplifies the notion of globalization being characterized by the *intensification* of flows that transcend national boundaries, which was referred to in Chapter 1 (Section 3.1). One way in which such flows are commonly examined is in terms of the *quantity*, or value, of cultural trade. Examining data on this we can see that the value of cultural imports and exports increased by nearly sixfold between 1970 and 1980, from about $6,800m. to $38,500m. (UNESCO, 1986, p.10). Whilst there are variations between countries and categories of cultural goods, *all* categories – printed matter, music, visual arts, cinema and photography, radio and television – show substantial growth.

The development and spread of information and communication technologies has been an important component of this growth – much of which has depended on the dramatic increase in the private ownership of communication hardware. The number of television receivers per thousand inhabitants in the world, for example, increased more than fourfold between 1965 and 1997, as shown in Table 2.1.

TABLE 2.1 World television receivers, 1965–97

Total number of receivers (millions)				Receivers per thousand inhabitants			
1965	1975	1985	1997	1965	1975	1985	1997
192	414	748	1,396	57	102	154	240

Sources: 1965 and 1975 data: UNESCO, 1989, Table 5.7; 1985 data: UNESCO, 1998, Table 6.5; 1997 data: UNESCO, 1999, Table IV.5.3

Unsurprisingly, the number of television households shows a similar growth. The graph in Figure 2.1 represents clearly the dramatic nature of the longitudinal picture.

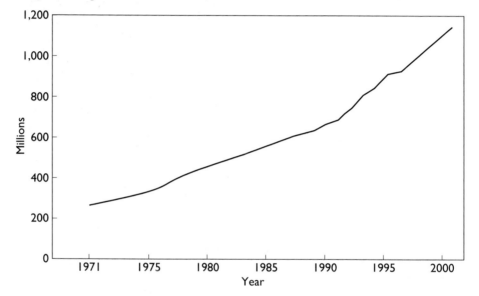

FIGURE 2.1   Global television households, 1971–2000

Source: *Screen Digest*, October 1996, p.225

This growth, like globalization generally as we saw in Chapter 1, is not an *even* process. Different regions of the world show enormous variations in both numbers and per capita ownership of televisions (see Table 2.2).

TABLE 2.2   Television receivers by region, 1997

	Total number of receivers (millions)	Receivers per 1,000 inhabitants
Africa	44	60
America	342	429
Asia	672	190
Europe	325	446
Oceania	12	427
World total	1,396	240

Source: UNESCO, 1999, Table IV.5.3

As you can see, there are most televisions in Asia, America and Europe, with Asia having around twice as many as Europe or America, and there are relatively few in Africa and Oceania. Per capita, however, we see Oceania, America and Europe with about 430 television receivers per 1,000 of the population, and Asia with under half that level and Africa with about one-seventh of this saturation.

FIGURE 2.2 Moving images coming to town: TV shop, Benin City, Nigeria

Different countries, as opposed to regions, show even wider disparities in levels of ownership. This is shown for television receivers and radios in relation to selected countries in Tables 2.3 and 2.4. These tables illustrate the disparities between nation-states, with data relating to the UK, the USA (one of the richest countries in the world), Burkina Faso (south of the Sahara, in West Africa, and one of the world's poorest countries), and China (a country with a huge population, and one showing a phenomenal rate of growth in ownership levels of television receivers).

TABLE 2.3 Television ownership and saturation in selected countries, 1975–97

	Total number of receivers (thousands)			Receivers per 1,000 inhabitants		
	1975	1985	1997	1975	1985	1997
Burkina Faso	9	37	100	1.5	4.7	9.1
China	1,185	69,650	400,000	1.3	65	321
UK	20,200	24,500	30,500	359	433	521
USA	121,000	190,000	219,000	560	786	806

Sources: 1975 data: UNESCO, 1994, Table 9.2; 1985 data: UNESCO, 1998, Table 9.2; 1997 data: UNESCO, 1999, Table IV.14

TABLE 2.4   Radio receiver ownership and saturation in selected countries, 1975–97

	Total number of receivers (thousands)			Receivers per 1,000 inhabitants		
	1975	1985	1997	1975	1985	1997
Burkina Faso	100	150	370	16	19	34
China	15,000	120,000	417,000	16	112	335
UK	39,000	57,000	84,500	694	1007	1,443
USA	401,000	500,000	575,000	1,857	2,067	2,116

Sources: 1975 data: UNESCO, 1994, Table 9.1; 1985 data: UNESCO, 1998, Table 9.1; 1997 data: UNESCO, 1999, Table IV.14

In addition to showing the enormous disparities between countries, you will have noticed that the data show that there has been a steady growth in the ownership of each of these technologies. As well as a growth of communication *hardware*, of some magnitude in most cases, recent years have seen a dramatic increase in the number of television *channels*. In the UK we have seen the emergence of Channels 4 and 5, of cable and satellite channels, and, most recently, of various digital channels. Such growth is taking place especially in Europe (see Figure 2.3) and North America.

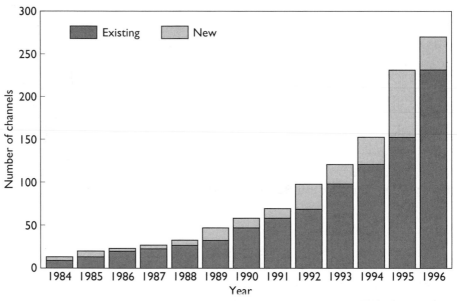

FIGURE 2.3   Growth of European television channels, 1984–96
Source: *Screen Digest*, March 1997, p.57

Cable and satellite have been responsible for the massive increase in demand for programming and in its growing global distribution. It was estimated that there would be a doubling of broadcast programme hours in Western Europe between 1986 and 2000 (Dyson and Humphreys, 1990).

With the proliferation of channels which are commercially funded – by advertising – there has been a decline in the market share of public television corporations (see Table 2.5). Whilst **public service broadcasting** isn't the only form of national broadcasting, its decline can be interpreted as a reduction in national broadcasting.

Public service broadcasting
A national broadcasting system which is available to all and insulated from the vested interests of government and corporations.

TABLE 2.5 Market share of public television corporations (by % share of viewing time)

	1975	1990	1995
Germany	100	68	39
Italy	91	51	48
France	100	34	41
Netherlands	100	56	39
UK	52	48	44

Sources: 1975 data: Barker, 1997, Table 2.1, p.32; 1990 and 1995 data: *Screen Digest*, April 1996, p.81

In the case of the UK, as you can see, the decline in BBC viewing is not great – in large part because since 1955 the BBC has operated in an environment which has included commercial television; and commercial television in the UK has been far more tightly regulated than elsewhere in the world, so is more like public service broadcasting than in (for example) the USA. As to whether (or how much) this will continue seems debatable. At the same time, of course, there has been a blurring between public and commercial broadcasting in various ways – for example, in the popularization of BBC news formats and content.

Thinking of your own television viewing, do you think that there are differences between ITV and BBC television channels? How would you characterize these differences? Do you think that BBC programming has changed in recent years?

Programming is largely about winning audiences (in the case of ITV to sell audiences to advertisers, and in the case of the BBC to justify the licence fee), and in the process we have seen no end of efforts by the BBC to produce popular material – soap opera, drama, sport and other genres – to meet consumer demand. At the same time, both have to maintain certain 'quality' requirements, but the BBC has to take account of its obligations in this respect as a public service broadcaster. So it operates with the tension of fulfilling this public service obligation and at the same time satisfying consumer demand: the BBC is neither immune from the logic of the market nor dismissive of viewers' preferences. Meanwhile ITV, with a lower budget to produce its programming, faces the tension between cost and quality – the latter required by the state regulator, the Independent Television Commission

(ITC). Despite the differences, there are many similarities and overlaps – and tensions, for example, with the recent loss by the BBC of its rights to broadcast key national sporting events.

Market competition has become severe, and there is considerable uncertainty about the future. Globally, cable grew from 83m. households in 1990 to 248m. in 1997, and in the UK from 149,000 to 2,374,000 in the same period (*Screen Digest*, April 1995, pp.86–8, and May 1998, p.111), so we are talking of very fast and large-scale growth. Like patterns of ownership of the various communication technologies, this process is not uniform across countries (see Figure 2.4).

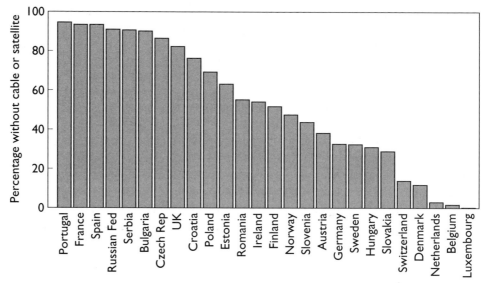

FIGURE 2.4   European households without cable or satellite, 1995

Source: *Screen Digest*, March 1997, p.59

Variations globally and even within Europe on the scale of public service broadcasting and the level of take-up of cable and satellite are fascinating and vast: at the end of the twentieth century, about a third of households in the UK had cable or satellite, compared with 12 per cent in France, and 98 per cent in the Netherlands. The reasons for this diversity are many and complex, and include the scale of indigenous production capability (which, in turn, is often related to the size of the state's population and its language and to a complex set of historical and cultural factors which have sustained local media production and consumption).

SUMMARY

- There are huge and fast-growing culture flows between countries.
- Ownership of televisions and radios has increased enormously worldwide, albeit with huge regional and national disparities.
- National broadcasting systems are experiencing declining audience shares.
- Cable and satellite ownership rates are increasing and in some countries are very high. They vary considerably between countries.

2.2 Positive globalists

Even in relation to the quantitative data, however, we can find considerable variation in the sense that is made of this information. Rather than speaking for themselves, the figures are open to a variety of interpretations. Globalists argue that the growth of global culture flows signals the demise of national cultures. Inter-nationalists – whose case we'll examine in Section 3 – are more sceptical, and focus on the continuity and strength of national cultures. Within the camp of the globalists we can distinguish between those who see the increasing global flow of communication and culture as 'a good thing', and those who see it as homogenizing or imperialist. We shall examine each of these briefly, starting with the optimists' analysis. We'll explore two very different types of 'positive globalist': those who focus on the progressive possibilities of the 'global village'; and liberal perspectives which point to the democratic nature of the free market and the benefits for viewers of greater choice.

The 'global village' is a notion which was developed by the media theorist Marshall McLuhan in the 1960s. It refers to the transcendance of constraints of physical place enabled by new communications technologies that allow instant, inexpensive, global communication. Although developed by a social scientist, the concept of the global village has become a powerful and popular metaphor for understanding the media in subsequent decades – it's a phrase you may well have heard – and in recent years it has enjoyed something of a revival. It has been put forward vociferously by those who extol the democratic and participatory possibilities afforded by the Internet.

Howard Rheingold, formerly associated with the 1960s' Californian counter-culture, a leading figure in the WELL, the Whole Earth 'Lectronic Link, an electronic community based in San Francisco, has articulated vociferously the progressive possibilities of the Internet (Rheingold, 1995). Rheingold draws on the work of the critical theorist Jurgen Habermas on the **public sphere** – space free from state control in which matters of polity and policy can be debated by citizens, a process and space which is seen as central to democracy. Rheingold follows Habermas in seeing around him the erosion of such free communication and discussion – with the growing manipulation of the news and public opinion by governments and corporations, through advertising, public relations and information management. Whereas television has become entertainment for profit, he sees the Internet as an electronic forum through which public opinion can be regenerated as citizens engage in rational argument. This is an argument which focuses on *structures* – structures of domination. Rheingold's interest is in how new electronic networks allow alternative structures, which bypass established institutions.

Public sphere
Space for public debate on polity and policy, which is free from government or institutional control.

Wherever computer mediated communication (CMC) becomes available to people, he says, virtual communities emerge, reflecting 'a hunger for community' (1995, p.6) in the context of the demise of the public sphere in our lives. The WELL, his electronic community, provides a context for the development of collective values and community. The Internet allows open, interactive, access – as opposed to the one-to-many nature of broadcasting systems. According to Rheingold, this allows for a greater diversity or plurality of voices to be heard, so is profoundly democratizing. On the Internet one can have truly global electronic communities, and new forms of participation, community and democracy.

With bulletin boards, websites and e-mail one can see the democratic possibilities of virtually free, instant multimedia communication. Their use by all manner of progressive organizations testifies to their utility in democratic processes. They allow a diversity of 'alternative' or radical voices to be accessed and heard – the Mexican Zapatistas movement's success has been attributed to its bypassing of 'official' media organizations by presenting its case to the world unmediated, on the Internet. If you can access the Internet, you may like to explore some of the sites of such 'alternative' organizations.

Turning to the *liberal enthusiasts of globalization*, we can identify those who see the market as itself democratizing, overcoming the elitism of *public service broadcasting* – meaning, in the case of the UK, the BBC. Some of these voices are those of the media industries, which benefit materially from the growth of channels and programming. But the liberal perspective is also prominent in government reports and underlies some key government policies on broadcasting. The Peacock Report (Home Office, 1986) played a crucial role in the **deregulation** of the UK media landscape, arguing that the public interest was best served by allowing consumers to act in their own best interests, free to choose what to watch. The sovereignty of the market is seen as a panacea for decisions being made about what we can watch by the cultural elitists who control the BBC.

Deregulation
Policies aimed at reducing state constraints (which were designed to serve the public or national interest) on the free market.

2.3 Pessimistic globalists

In academia, however, we find more critical and pessimistic (or realistic?) interpretations of the globalization of culture. We shall explore three such analyses. First, is the argument that we are witnessing increasing inequalities of access to the hardware and software whereby culture is distributed and communicated. Second, we shall examine the increasingly concentrated ownership of media corporations, which have globalized and developed interests which span the leisure, entertainment and information sectors. This illustrates the argument in Chapter 1 (Section 3.1) that globalization is about *stretching*, that processes increasingly stretch across national boundaries and to distant parts of the globe. Finally – and this is the main focus of this section – we shall look at some approaches to *cultural imperialism*, examining the argument that global culture is in fact Western culture, and that this is disseminated globally to bolster the economic interests of the West or the USA.

2.3.1   Growing inequalities

Although Rheingold argues that more communication makes for a better world, contemporary developments can be seen less positively. The growth in the ownership and use of communication technologies and in global communication is taking place at the same time as a dramatic increase in global inequalities. These inequalities can be illustrated in a whole host of ways. They are clearly manifest – as we have seen – in patterns of ownership of domestic communication devices and in the access enjoyed to information and communications services.

Notions of community are a far cry from the growing inequalities within and between nations and the increasing fragmentation and segmentation of society. The growth of global communication and culture flows has little to do with levelling the playing field, with reducing global inequalities. To the contrary, it has coincided with the reproduction and exacerbation of the inequalities that characterize the contemporary era. More than this, there is a growing gulf between those with an increasing array of information devices and sources – the 'information rich' – and the 'information poor' who lack electricity, communication technologies or access to information.

2.3.2   Concentration of ownership

The second body of literature to recognize but criticize the globalization of culture focuses on the increasing concentration of ownership of the media, and the totalitarian possibilities of the increasingly homogenized nature of the media. Examining the structures of organization and control leads to a concern that fewer voices can be heard, despite the proliferation of media output. Recent years have seen a dramatic concentration in the ownership of global media and culture organizations, as well as a growth in the circulation and penetration of their products. This is an example of a growing transnational *infrastructure* which bypasses the nation-state, referred to in Chapter 1 (Section 3.1) as a key feature of globalization. The global media market is dominated by 10 transnational corporations, the names of many of which may be familiar to you – Time Warner, Disney, Bertelsmann, Viacom, Tele-Communications Inc, News Corporation, Sony, Seagram (formerly Universal), General Electric (formerly NBC), and Dutch Phillips (formerly Polygram). There are tremendous advantages of scale, so the field is characterized by mergers, acquisitions and joint ventures – and we can reasonably predict that there will have been more of these by the time you read this. These increasingly large and powerful organizations are controlling distribution as well as content, in a situation of rapid flux and uncertainty.

The significance of such corporations in the global economy is indicated by their growing presence in the FT500, the list of the largest companies in the world. In 1998, Microsoft was ranked number 3, Disney 40, Sony 75, Time

Warner 96, Reuters 183 and News Corporation 408 (*Financial Times*, 22 January 1998, pp.5–6).

News Corporation, perhaps best known in the UK for its ownership of *The Sun* newspaper, has joint ventures with each of the other top 10 corporations. Moreover, its interests increasingly span hardware as well as software, and a breadth of leisure and entertainment businesses as well as the media.

You probably know that Murdoch's News International owns *The Sun*. But what other components of his empire can you name?

A brief account of Murdoch's global media empire gives an indication of its far-reaching scale and nature. You may find yourself surprised at the breadth of Murdoch's interests.

ACTIVITY 2.1

As you read the following account of News Corporation, consider and note why the scale and scope of Murdoch's empire is relevant to issues of culture and democracy.

News Corporation's interests

The five largest media firms in the world in terms of sales – Time Warner, Disney, Bertelsmann, Viacom, and News Corporation – are also the most fully integrated global media giants. [...]

Although News Corporation ranks fifth with approximately $10 billion in 1996 sales, it provides the archetype for the twenty-first century global media firm in many respects [...]. The News Corporation is often identified with its head, Rupert Murdoch, whose family controls some 30 per cent of its stock. [...]

After establishing News Corporation in his native Australia, Murdoch entered the British market in the 1960s and by the 1980s had become a dominant force in the US market. [...]

News Corporation's more significant media holdings include the following:

- Some 132 newspapers (primarily in Australia, Britain, and the United States), making it one of the three largest newspaper groups in the world;

- Twentieth Century Fox, a major film, television and video production center, which has a library of over 2,000 films to exploit;

- The US Fox broadcasting network;

- Twenty-two US television stations, the largest US station group, covering over 40 per cent of US TV households;

- Twenty-five magazines, most notably *TV Guide*;

- Book-publishing interests, including Harper Collins;

- A 50 per cent stake (with TCI's Liberty Media) in several US and global cable networks, including fX, fXM, Fox Sports Net;

- Fox News Channel;

- Asian Star Television, satellite service and television channels;

- Controlling interest (40 per cent) in British Sky Broadcasting (BSkyB) (1996 sales: $1.6 billion);

- BSkyB has a 4 per cent stake in UK's Granada Sky Television satellite channel group;

- A 49.9 per cent stake in Germany's Vox channel;

- A 30 per cent stake in Sky Latin America digital satellite service;

- A 40 per cent stake in US Sky Television, a digital satellite joint venture with Echostar and Concert;

- A 50 per cent stake in Japan Sky Broadcasting digital satellite service;

- Australian Foxtel cable channel;

- A 49.9 per cent stake in India's Zee TV;

- The Spanish-language El Canal Fox in Latin America;

- UK Sky Radio;

- A 15 per cent stake in the Australian Seven networks;

- India Sky Broadcasting digital satellite service;

- A 50 per cent stake in channel V, Asian music video channel;

- A 45 per cent stake in Hong Kong-based Phoenix Satellite Television Company. [...]

News Corporation operates in nine different media on six continents. In 1995 its revenues were distributed relatively evenly between filmed entertainment (26 per cent), newspapers (24 per cent), television (21 per cent), magazines (14 per cent), and book publishing (12 per cent). [...] News Corporation earned 70 per cent of its 1995 income in the United States and 17 per cent in Britain. Most of the balance came from Australia and Asia.

News Corporation's plan for global expansion looks to the areas where growth is expected to be greatest for commercial media: continental Europe, Asia and Latin America. [...]

News Corporation is almost as concerned with producing content as with owning distribution channels. Aside from tried-and-tested filmed entertainment and music videos, the 'sure-fire winners' in global television are news, animation and sports.

Source: Herman and McChesney, 1997, pp.70–2, 75

C O M M E N T

Clearly, News Corporation, like other global media conglomerates, is a major business. Its significance, however, is far greater than suggested by its scale or reach – because of the crucial *symbolic and cultural significance* of its product. This is why, for centuries, there has been state regulation of the media. The potentially anti-democratic nature of ownership patterns is clear. Murdoch, for example, was reluctant for any wing of his empire to criticize China in the context of his aspirations for Star TV in that country; more recently, there was considerable concern when he tried to buy Manchester United FC.

The concentrated pattern of media ownership has profound consequences for media forms. With the growth of advertising-financed services, audience maximization has become increasingly important in shaping programming. The outcome has been not a greater range or quality of programming, but the reverse – and allegations of '57 channels but nothing on' and 'wall-to-wall *Dallas*', as the multiplicity of channels on the network simultaneously seek to woo the same audience, pitching their programming at a limited section of the population. This is a far cry from the diversity and choice extolled by liberal globalists.

2.3.3 Cultural imperalism

Cultural imperialism, a major focus of this chapter, is perhaps the longest-established theory for explaining cultural globalization, and we shall now explore some of the diverse issues and arguments it encompasses. Cultural imperialism is rooted in a common-sense notion many of us understand: that the reduction in cultural differences around the world – for example, that France does not seem as distinctive as it did 30 years ago – is *because of* the distribution by global corporations of commodified Western culture, a process which has *worked to the advantage* of the USA and Western nations.

Not confined to common sense, this is an argument rooted in the work of the Frankfurt School of sociology. By this is meant in particular the work of Theodor Adorno and Max Horkheimer, German Jewish academics who fled to the USA in the 1930s, where they continued their work on the homogenization of culture and the authoritarian domination which they saw as characterizing capitalism. Focusing on manipulation, their argument is structural, and concerned with the commodification of culture – they saw culture as something which, increasingly, is bought and sold, a part of the market system. Acknowledgement of cultural imperialism can be seen as the rationale behind the United Nations Education, Scientific and Cultural Organization (UNESCO)'s calls for a 'new world information and communication order' and its policies on global culture (McBride, 1980). Culture flows are profoundly imbalanced, and dominant cultures are seen as threatening more vulnerable cultures. This is a matter of the *interpenetration* of the global and local referred to as a dimension of globalization in Chapter 1 (Section 3.1), focusing as it does on the local becoming more globally integrated. UNESCO's approach draws on Lenin's analysis of imperialism and on a diversity of other strands, including popular concerns about 'Americanization' – the malign influence of American cultural exports to Europe, a phenomenon which can be traced back to the presence in the UK of US troops in the Second World War (Hebdige, 1988). UNESCO's concern has been with the inequality of flows – from North to South and from core to periphery. News, for example, is gathered, selected and controlled by Western corporations, as a commodity for profit, rather than as a means of development. Five major Western news agencies are responsible for 80 per cent of the world's news, and only a quarter of world news is about developing countries (Masmoudi, 1979). The cultural imperialism thesis is associated primarily with the work of Herbert Schiller (for example, Schiller, 1991). It foregrounds something which is obvious and incontrovertible – that 'global culture' is not something which draws in any even or uniform way on the vast diversity of cultures in the world, balancing or synthesizing these, but, rather, consists of the global dissemination of US or Western culture – the complete opposite of diversity.

> **" It doesn't matter whether it comes in by cable, telephone lines, computer, or satellite. Everyone's going to have to deal with Disney. "**
> Disney Chairman and Chief Executive Officer Michael Eisner

FIGURE 2.5
The onslaught of Disney

ACTIVITY 2.2

Given your understanding and experience of national cultures and identities note how Coca-Cola, Disney or McDonald's might be seen as reinforcing or undermining national cultures and identities. Then consider debates on power (e.g. **Allen, 2004**) and note who you see as the beneficiaries of the operations of these corporations.

FIGURE 2.6   The global reach of Coca-Cola: quenching the thirst in Phnom Penh

COMMENT

Clearly, these are big areas of debate and complex questions of enormous contemporary relevance. At the time of writing, French farmers are attacking McDonald's because they see it as emblematic of American culture and imports. As well as supplying consumers with food and drink for which there is a high demand, such powerful corporations are organized to benefit their shareholders (mostly in the USA) and are a highly visible symbol of US involvement in national economies throughout the world.

According to the cultural imperialism thesis, global cultural flows are not a part of a civilizing or development process but, much less benignly or symmetrically, involve cultural imposition and dominance. Some see this as having become exacerbated with the demise of the Eastern bloc and the rise of the World Bank, World Trade Organization and International Monetary Fund, which have operated to increase inequalities. Clearly, this is an analysis which focuses on broader structures.

There is considerable data to support the cultural imperialism argument. By and large I'm sure you would agree that most of what passes as 'global culture' – Coca-Cola, McDonald's, Levi's, Disney, MTV or Hollywood – emanates from the USA. The vast and intrusive presence of US cultural goods seems undeniable. On a global level the majority of imported television programmes originate in the USA, and, less so, Western Europe and Japan. In some regions of the world, for example Latin America, three-quarters of imported television originates in the USA (Varis, 1985). Rupert Murdoch and Bill Gates aren't aiming to subject populations worldwide to imperial dictates, but are trying to persuade them to buy their products, which span the communication hardware and software, information, leisure and entertainment sectors. Colonialism today can thus be seen as based on a new set of products, which focus on the electronic communications media. We'll now examine some of the evidence for the cultural imperialism thesis.

Of worldwide exports of programming hours, over 40 per cent come from the USA. Of those imported by Europe, 44 per cent are from the USA. Of imports to Latin America, 77 per cent are from the USA. In the case of Canada, 70 per cent of imports are from the USA; and for Africa south of the Sahara, 47 per cent (Varis, 1984, 1985). Conversely, the USA imports 1 per cent of its commercial programming and 2 per cent of its public service programming. This seems a clear and dramatic picture.

Language, of course, is central to this patterning, with English the 'language of advantage' (Collins, 1990, p.211) by dint of US imperialism and the historical legacy of Europe and the British Empire. A great proportion of the world's scientific knowledge and formally codified information is in English, which is also the main language for communication within and between global organizations and institutions. Data on translation confirms this overwhelming primacy of English, the language not just of large numbers, but of relatively affluent people. Moreover, it is the second language of much of the rest of the world's population, spoken by about a quarter of the human race. In the mid 1980s, English was the original language of 47 per cent of the world's translations, compared with Spanish as the original language for 1.5 per cent, and Chinese for 0.3 per cent of translations (Therborn, 1995). This domination of the English language is, of course, an example of homogenization, the opposite of diversity.

So there is considerable evidence to support the notion that the globalization of culture is not the emergence and growth of a global culture, but a spreading in the English language of US or Western cultural goods and practices. Recognition of this has been translated into polices banning satellite dishes in Iran; and the imposition of tariffs or quotas on imported music, film or television, for example in France.

Under the umbrella of such arguments one can find interesting coalitions of the 'left' (opposed to profit-motivated global corporate capital) and the 'right' (defending national culture). For the 'left', liberal deregulation of the media is seen as masquerading as freedom of choice, but in reality is clearing the ground

DORFMAN & MATTELART

HOW TO READ DONALD DUCK

IG
$3.25
£1.35

NATIONAL
BANK
DEPOSITOS
NOCTURNOS

IMPERIALIST IDEOLOGY
IN THE DISNEY
COMIC

for colonization by capitalist corporate culture. For the 'right', Disney is ersatz culture that corrupts or threatens distinct and historically rooted cultural traditions and practices.

More than an account of cultural domination, however, cultural imperialism links explicitly the cultural policies and practices of the USA and Western nations with the economic interests of these same countries. So it is a *structural* explanation. Cultural domination is seen as a part of a strategy to generate demand for Western goods and to compound subordination and inequality between producer and recipient cultures. Mattelart's work on Disney has been particularly influential in this context, arguing that Donald Duck caricatures and deprecates 'Third World' cultures and consistently carries messages on how 'Third World' people should aspire to live. Thus, he links cultural imperialism to the interests and spread of global corporate capitalism (Dorfman and Mattelart, 1975; Mattelart *et al.*, 1984).

FIGURE 2.7   The imperialist ideology of Donald Duck: the front cover of Dorfman and Mattelart's *How to Read Donald Duck* (1975)

SUMMARY

Globalists tend to focus on structures, and argue that the growth of global culture flows signals the demise of national cultures.

Positive globalists see this as a welcome development:

● 'Global villagers' argue that with the Internet we have the possibility of a revitalized public sphere and a restoration of communities, with open access and many-to-many global communication.

● Other positive globalists argue, from a liberal perspective, that the public interest is best served not by empowering the cultural elite which runs the BBC, but by allowing consumers freedom of choice.

Pessimistic globalists argue that:

● Globalization is not a levelling or increasing of uniformity, but the reproduction and extension of inequalities between nations.

- Global media and cultural corporations are massive structures and have become an increasingly significant component of the global economy. They are closely linked with one another and have interests that span the breadth of the information, communication, entertainment and leisure sectors.

- 'Cultural imperialism' is an important way of understanding the globalization of culture. This is a structural analysis which has at its core two notions: that dominant cultures of the West and the USA are swamping minority cultures in processes of homogenization, reducing diversity; and that this is a strategy to meet the economic interests of the USA and other Western nations.

3 INTER-NATIONALISTS

No-one seriously argues that nothing has changed, that national cultures continue unchanged in the context of cultural globalization. It *is* argued, however, that the claims for globalization are excessive in that they ignore important ways in which key cultural forms and institutions remain deeply national. From this perspective, cultural imperialism is seen as overstating external structural forces and undervaluing internal, local, dynamics and human agency; and as overstating change and relegating continuities.

Inter-nationalists root their argument in the durability of the local, and of nation-states. Anthony Smith (1995), a leading writer on nationalism, addresses the depth and history of national cultures. Albeit culturally constructed, they are the outcome of centuries of continuity, communication, interaction and collective experience, forged in history, closely linked with identities and not easily replaced or redirected. Compared with deep-rooted and long-standing national cultures, Disney and the like may earn profits, but they are ephemeral, they don't connect with everyday lives and identities as do national cultures.

We'll examine briefly four examples of powerful national continuities – public service broadcasting, the press, the news, and systems of regulation. The section will conclude by examining the telegraph, a case study which suggests that we should be cautious of those who claim that everything has changed dramatically, that we live in apocalyptic times. The telegraph in the Victorian era (and especially between 1850 and 1860) may have been a more dramatic transformation of the world than we are experiencing with the Internet today.

3.1   National and global television audiences

The public service broadcaster in the UK is the BBC. Whilst the audience share of public service broadcasting varies dramatically between countries, in the UK the arrival of ITV in the mid 1950s in some senses paved the way for a relatively responsive and competitive form of public service broadcasting. The impact of cable and satellite on broadcasting in the UK is far less dramatic than in some other countries, with public service broadcasting remaining resilient in the face of global challenges. Nor is the UK unique: in Australia ABC has improved ratings, and in Italy RAI channels beat the combined commercial channels (Barker, 1997).

In the UK in 1999, only about a third of households had cable or satellite, and in these households, cable and satellite channels account for only just over a third of television viewing. This contrasts strongly with the hyperbole which has surrounded digital, cable and satellite television, and should caution us to be wary of some of the claims which are being made for these new distribution technologies. Table 2.6 shows the distribution of audience in the UK between national and global television channels.

TABLE 2.6   Estimated audience share for national and global television channels in the UK, 1997

Channel	Percentage in all households[a]	Percentage in satellite and cable homes[b]
Total BBC	44	31.1
Total terrestrial commercial	45.5	32.1
Total non-terrestrial	10.5	36.7
Total BSkyB	4.9	16.8
MTV	0.2	0.8
Nickelodeon	0.5	1.8
Country Music Television	0.1	0.1
Discovery Channel (Europe)	0.2	1.2
The Disney Channel	0.3	0.8
The Paramount Channel	0.1	0.3
Fox Kids	–	0.3

[a] For year ending 31 December 1996 (ITC, 1997)
[b] For week ending 29 June 1997 (Phillips, 1997, p.30)
Source: Sparks, 1998, Table 6.1, p.116

As you can see, the audiences for truly global television – for example, MTV and Disney channels – are minuscule. In the UK, these attract respectively 0.2 per cent and 0.3 per cent of the total television audience – compared with 44 per cent for BBC (of which 11.5 per cent is BBC2 and 32.5 per cent BBC1). In the UK, the top 40 programmes in terms of audience size in a sample week were domestically produced; the first import was *Neighbours* at number 41, and in the top 70 were only eight programmes from abroad, all from Australia (data from Phillips, 1997, cited and analysed by Sparks, 1998).

MTV Europe and Star television in India provide examples of the limits of globalization – in each case, consumers rejected global broadcasting and this had to be replaced with domestically produced material. Indeed, BSkyB is best understood as a UK company. Murdoch's is a global empire; BSkyB is transmitted by a satellite that is based in Luxembourg, and its footprint is an area that extends beyond the UK. On the other hand, its news is British, it has a negligible audience share beyond the UK, and it is regulated by the UK Independent Television Commission (ITC).

Globally, broadcast material which is domestically produced is 29 times greater in volume than that which crosses national borders (O'Regan 1992; cited by Sinclair *et al.*, 1996). This leads some commentators to conclude that 'Television is still a gloriously hybrid medium, with a plethora of programming of an inescapably and essentially local, untranslatable nature' (Sinclair *et al.*, 1996, p.10).

3.2 The press

In the UK, perhaps the most obvious – almost the only – examples of a global press are the *Financial Times* and the *Wall Street Journal*. With the exception of the *Wall Street Journal*, the UK's press is domestically produced. Indeed, over 90 per cent of daily newspapers sold in Scotland are produced in Scotland; and the *Glasgow Herald* and the *Scotsman* outsell the total of London-based qualities in Scotland. The *Financial Times* has a circulation of 130,000 outside Europe, with an average income of $120,000. The *Wall Street Journal* has a European circulation of 64,000, with an average income of $196,000. In the UK, where it faces competition from the *Financial Times*, the *Wall Street Journal* has one-thirteenth the circulation of the *Financial Times*, which demonstrates readers' preferences for local media where this is available. The global circulation of these two newspapers is

FIGURE 2.8 The limits of a global press: *Financial Times* readers have an average annual income of approximately £120,000

extremely small and their readers are extremely rich. The media theorist Colin Sparks concludes that:

> On a generous interpretation ... we may say that the evidence of globalization in the mass media is weak. Some media have made some steps in that direction, but their total audiences are very small and are completely dwarfed by the scale of audiences for purely state-based media ...
>
> ... the audience for these new 'global' media are disproportionately amongst the elite, and need to understand a world language (notably English or Spanish), either as native speakers or as an additional tongue, in order to benefit from this material. If there is an emerging 'CNN-watching, *Time*-reading international professional class', it is very small in numbers, very rich compared with the majority of the population of the advanced countries, and is sufficiently well-educated as to be so entirely at home with English that it is capable of reading material that even the majority of native speakers find too difficult for easy consumption. Neither is there strong evidence that these emerging global media are seriously eroding the national media. The audiences for the state-based press and broadcasting alter without apparent relationship to the development or otherwise of whatever global media happen to be available.
>
> (Sparks, 1998, p.119)

3.3   News

Clearly, newsgathering has become globalized in a variety of ways, notably by using satellite links to increase the immediacy of distant news – most prominently in the Gulf War. There has been a quite dramatic growth of global news services and agencies, such as Reuters. But our news is produced almost entirely within the UK. CNN is not a global broadcasting organization, but better seen as one providing a US service with a little international content. In any case, CNN International is available in only 113m. households worldwide, a tiny share of available or national broadcasting audiences. The *daily* reach of ITV and BBC prime time news combined is greater than the *monthly* reach of CNN *throughout Europe* (Sparks, 1998).

3.4   Regulation

Systems or structures of regulation are also predominantly national and – notwithstanding the EU, General Agreement on Tariffs and Trade (GATT), and the World Trade Organization (WTO) – remain powerful and important determinants of cultural circulation. It is sometimes argued that new technologies such as satellite make national regulation outdated and impossible. But satellite broadcasting – in the UK and elsewhere – *is* subject to national regulation. Under the 1990 Broadcasting Act, satellite services can be proscribed and penalties imposed. The UK government has excluded successfully pornography channels based in countries with less restrictions on standards in broadcasting. Clearly, however, the future is uncertain, with increasing liberal pressures on governments to reduce their regulation of the media in the 'public interest'.

3.5 What's new? The Victorian Internet

Tom Standage, a technology journalist, argues that the real shrinking of time and space took place not with the arrival of the Internet but in the Victorian era with the development of the telegraph.

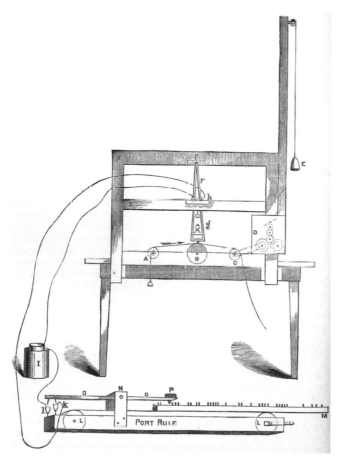

FIGURE 2.9 Samuel Morse's telegraph: a device that changed the world. In this original version, turning a handle in the sending apparatus (bottom) moved a toothed rack, making and breaking an electrical circuit. In the receiver (above), the intermittent current was recorded as a zigzag line on a moving tape by deflecting a pencil with an electromagnet

Around the middle of the nineteenth century it was widely felt that the telegraph would unite humanity because, for the first time, communication could take place faster than the speed of a person on a horse or at sea. Newspapers were able to report events taking place on the other side of the world within hours of their occurrence, instead of waiting perhaps years for an expedition to return. This changed dramatically views of the world.

The enthusiasm – and investment – which the technology engendered is quite remarkable. After linking London to Paris in 1852, attempts were made to lay a 2,500-mile cable to the USA. In 1857, two cable-laying ships left Valentia Island in south-west Ireland, but the cable broke after 350 miles. More money was raised and about a year later two ships sailed to the middle of the Atlantic and headed in opposite directions laying the cable. Twice the cable snapped and they sailed back to the starting point; and an encounter with a whale and one more break meant abandoning the venture and a return to Ireland. On the next attempt they achieved success, connecting the two continents by cable in 1858:

> The celebrations that followed bordered on hysteria. There were hundred-gun salutes in Boston and New York; flags flew from public buildings; church bells rang. There were fireworks, parades, and special church services. Torchbearing revellers in New York got so carried away that City Hall was accidentally set on fire and narrowly escaped destruction.
>
> 'Our whole country', declared *Scientific American*, 'has been electrified by the successful laying of the Atlantic Telegraph.'
>
> (Standage, 1998, pp.77, 79)

Queen Victoria and President James Buchanan sent messages; Tiffany's, the New York jewellers, bought the leftover cable and made commemorative souvenirs; books were published on the feat; poems were written; sermons given relating the event to biblical stories; and *The Times* echoed others by saying that the cable had reunited the British and American peoples: 'The Atlantic is dried up, and we become in reality as well as in wish one country. The Atlantic Telegraph has half undone the Declaration of 1776, and has gone far to make us once again, in spite of ourselves, one people' (cited in Standage, 1998, pp.80–1). Morse, the hero of the technology, was the recipient of honours and awards around the world. He and his invention were said to have united the people of the world, promoted world peace, revolutionized commerce, widened the range of human thought and improved the standard of literature.

Standage's conclusion is that the perceived significance of the telegraph resembles closely that of the Internet:

> it revolutionised business practice, gave rise to new forms of crime, and inundated its users with a deluge of information. Romance blossomed over the wires. Secret codes were devised by some users, and cracked by others. The benefits of the network were relentlessly hyped by its advocates, and dismissed by the sceptics.

Governments and regulators tried and failed to control the new medium. Attitudes to everything from newsgathering to diplomacy had to be completely rethought. Meanwhile, out on the wires, a technological subculture with its own customs and vocabulary was establishing itself.

(Standage, 1998, p.1)

He argues that the electric telegraph was much more disconcerting for the people of its age than are new communication technologies today: 'If any generation has the right to claim that it bore the full bewildering, world-shrinking brunt of such a revolution, it is not us – it is our nineteenth-century forebears' (Standage, 1998, pp.199–200).

SUMMARY

Inter-nationalists do not argue that nothing has changed, but point to powerful continuities for national media and the continuing significance of local and national cultural production and consumption.

- Public service, national broadcasting is alive and well, albeit with reduced audiences, under increasing pressure to compete, and in an environment which is uncertain and fast-changing.

- In the UK in 1999, about a third of households had cable or satellite television, and they watched *terrestrial* channels for nearly two-thirds of their viewing time.

- There is hardly such a thing as 'global television'. What there is attracts minimal audiences.

- Viewing figures, however, are not the whole story, because commercial forms and practices are influencing heavily the content of national broadcasting organizations.

- The press is profoundly national in its organization.

- News, although globally sourced, is almost entirely nationally or locally produced.

- The nation-state remains the main body which regulates the media.

- The history of the telegraph suggests that there is nothing dramatically new about recent communication technologies and global communication, and cautions us regarding the more apocalyptic claims which are made about 'the information revolution'.

4   TRANSFORMATIONALISTS

So far, we have seen both some continuities for national cultures, but also some transformations, in the form of increasing global cultural flows. The evidence suggests that we can't say that 'it's all as it was', nor that 'everything has changed'. Between these two extremes, however, there is a body of research evidence which suggests that some important changes have taken place, but that these changes, and their consequences, are rather more nuanced or contradictory than suggested by either inter-nationalists or globalists.

4.1   Culture flows are not simply one-way

Perhaps the most prominent critique of globalists by transformationalists is that the cultural imperialism thesis is a US-centric story. It focuses on the dissemination by a power elite of ideas and ways of thinking, and on a one-way flow. In so doing, it ignores much of the evidence about international culture flows and, in particular, countervailing flows – for example, the phenomenon of 'world music'. It ignores the fact that heavy importers of US programming include strong regional exporters. And it ignores the very important and substantial regional flows – for example of *telenovelas*, Latin American soap operas which are exported to the USA and Europe. Developing this line of argument, Sinclair *et al.* see the world as divided into a number of 'geolinguistic' regions, each with its own internal dynamics as well as global links:

> global, regional, national, and even local circuits of programmed exchange overlap and interact in a multi-faceted way ... Instead of the image of 'the West' at the centre dominating the peripheral 'Third World' with an outward flow of cultural products, this [approach] ... sees the world as divided into a number of regions which each have their own internal dynamics as well as their global ties. Although primarily based on geographic realities, these regions are also defined by common cultural, linguistic, and historical connections which transcend physical space. Such a dynamic, regionalist view of the world helps us to analyse in a more nuanced way the intricate and multi-directional flows of television across the globe.
>
> (Sinclair et al., 1996, p.5)

Figure 2.10 indicates the scale and direction of the import of television programming, and indicates something of the complexity of this flow. As Sinclair *et al.* argue, it is important to distinguish not just 'local' from 'global',

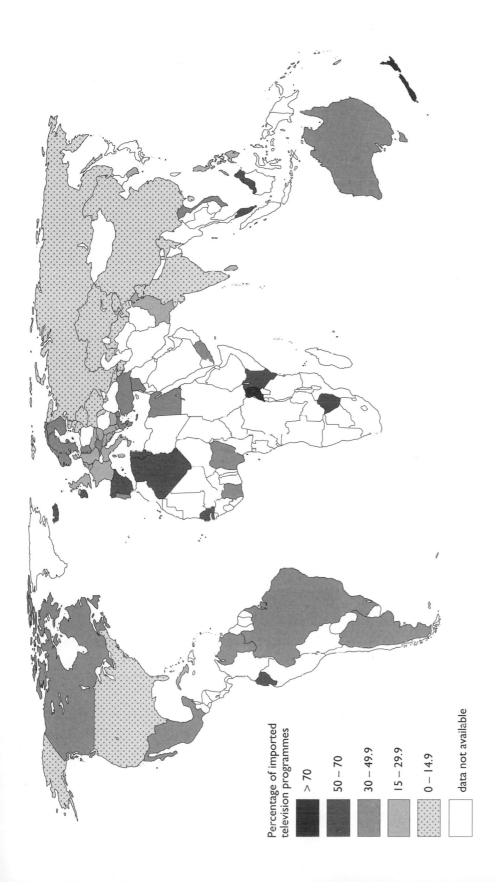

FIGURE 2.10 Percentage of imported television programmes in selected countries, 1983. (*Note*: Where percentages for more than one TV channel within a country are available, an average has been calculated by adding these percentages and dividing the total by the number of channels)

Source of data: Varis, 1985, Table 4, pp.19–21

Percentage of imported
television programmes

> 70

50 – 70

30 – 49.9

15 – 29.9

0 – 14.9

data not available

but also 'regional' from 'global'. Such regional trading is based on common language and culture and historical trading links, and contributes to an 'imagined community' which – in the case of *telenovelas* – encompasses US cable networks, Portugal and Spain as well as Latin America. Such flows are a major element of the international traffic of television programming, which constitutes a complex picture.

It has been argued that to understand global television flows we need to distinguish between countries that have no need to import programmes because they have their own production facilities (e.g. the UK, Brazil, Japan); those that need additional programming to fill their schedules (e.g. Canada, Australia); and those with little domestic production (e.g. countries in Africa and Asia, except India) (Cantor and Cantor, 1992). We would also need to distinguish between types of programme – the USA, for example, exports predominantly fiction. Finally, we would need to consider the duration of flow – for example, whether a high level of cultural imports is to kick-start an indigenous industry, to be replaced at a later date by domestic production, as was the case with US exports to Latin America in the 1960s.

4.2   The audience for imported television

Perhaps most importantly, we need to examine audience ratings, to see how many people are watching indigenous and imported programmes. Interestingly, audience research shows that, throughout the world, domestically produced programmes attract the highest audiences and are transmitted at peak viewing times. US imports commonly fill the less popular time slots. This is hardly surprising, because if a programme is to appeal to a global audience it almost *requires* a lack of a strong specific cultural reference. So rather than a process – let alone a strategy – of cultural domination, much of the global flow of television is simply a consequence of the increase in transmission hours and the demand for cheap material to fill the less popular slots. Clearly, this raises doubts about the cultural impact of imported programming. Quite simply, volume does not equate with cultural significance.

4.3   Cultural purity and cultural swamping

Implicit in the arguments of the cultural imperialism thesis is the assumption that the authentic culture of recipient nations – many of them in the developing world – is being eroded by inauthentic, ersatz, imposed culture. It is at least implicit that culture is defined in national terms, within which it is reasonably integrated and homogeneous. This raises the interesting and difficult question of who defines and represents a nation's culture. Defending cultural identity against the supposed threat of cultural imperialism necessarily involves invoking partial notions of national identity. Defending 'Englishness', 'Frenchness', or 'Welshness', for example, has the effect of regulating internally cultural identity by relegating the nation's ethnic and cultural diversity (Tomlinson, 1997). At least implicitly, it assumes an outdated homogeneity of national culture, in an era in which nations are characterized, instead, by cultural hybridity and 'creolism' – by which is meant that, as a result of the interaction of two cultures, often on unequal terms, over an extended period of time, new cultural forms emerge which aren't simply derived from one or other culture (Hannerz, 1990).

4.4 Reading culture

Finally, there is the question of the *significance* of the consumption of imported culture. Proponents of the cultural imperialism thesis such as Mattelart and Schiller have tended to rest their argument on assumptions about impact, about how audiences 'read' – or **decode** – cultural texts. (By a cultural 'text' I mean anything which can be 'read', made sense of, interpreted by an audience or consumer.) They tend to assume that viewing Western capitalist television entails the inculcation of Western values, particularly regarding consumer desires. So how *is* imported television used, what sense *is* made of it, and how does this process of consumption shape, or intersect with, everyday lives and routines?

Decode
The process whereby users or consumers *make sense* of cultural texts.

ACTIVITY 2.3

Table 2.7 overleaf is an extract from a newspaper TV guide showing programmes on three TV channels in Papua New Guinea. If you are familiar with any of the programmes listed, consider their possible significance in Papua New Guinea by answering the following questions.

- What sorts of values are implicit in the programmes?

- How might the programmes be relevant to the Papua New Guinea context?

- Imagine large audiences for the programmes over an extended period of time. Do you think that the programmes could have any long-term consequences for identities and communities in Papua New Guinea?

TABLE 2.7   Papua New Guinea TV listings

EMTV		CENTRAL		ABC	
5.30	JOYCE MEYER MINISTRY: "Life in the Word". (G)	6.00	THE BIG BREAKFAST	6.00	LIFE LONG LEARNING: "Growing Awareness". (G)
6.00	EARLY NEWS: (G)	8.30	THE BOOK PLACE: (G)		
7.00	TODAY SHOW: (G)	9.00	A COUNTRY PRACTICE: (PG)	6.00	PRESERVE THE LEGACY
9.00	BENNY HINN MINISTRY: "This is Your Day".(G)	10.00	DENISE: (G)	7.30	TELETUBBIES: (G)
		11.00	HOME AND AWAY	8.00	JOHNSON: (G)
9.30	***TEST PATTERN***	12.00	MOVIE: "Blind Fear". A blind woman tries to outwit three gangsters holing up at an isolated lodge. (M)	8.30	SESAME STREET
12.00	3RD TEST CRICKET: "Australia vs Pakistan"			9.25	BANANAS IN PYJAMAS: (G)
2.30	KIDS KONA: "Sesame Street".(G)			9.30	PLAY SCHOOL: (G)
3.30	SUPERMAN *Final* (G)			10.00	RAT-A-TAT-TAT
4.00	WONDER WORLD: (G)	2.00	RICKI LAKE: (PG)	10.30	NATURALLY AUSTRALIA
4.30	TOTALLY WILD: (G)	3.00	I DREAM OF JEANNIE	10.45	THE TEXT FILES
4.57	EMTV TOKSAVE WITH DORRIS: (G)	3.30	DISNEY ADVENTURES	11.00	HAZARDS, DISASTERS & SURVIVAL
		4.00	CHUCK FINN		
5.00	HOME AND AWAY: (G)	4.30	MARY TYLER MOORE SHOW	11.30	BEHIND THE NEWS
5.29	EMTV NEWS BREAK: (G)			12.00	WORLD AT NOON
5.30	NEIGHBOURS: (G)	5.00	HUEY'S COOKING: (G)	12.30	BEST OF AUSTRALIA
6.00	NATIONAL EMTV NEWS: (G)	5.30	SONS & DAUGHTERS	1.00	THE TOP FLOOR
		6.00	HOME AND AWAY	2.00	PARLIAMENT QUESTION TIME
6.30	CURRENT AFFAIRS: (G)	6.30	WHEEL OF FORTUNE		
6.59	NEWS UPDATE	7.00	SEVEN NIGHTLY NEWS	3.00	SESAME STREET (G)
7.00	LOTTO DRAW	7.30	THE GREAT SOUTH EAST	3.20	PLAY SCHOOL: (G)
7.01	KIDS SAY THE DARNDEST THINGS: Join comedian Bill Cosby as he chats openly with everyday young people. You'll be amazed at some of the things kids say ...(G)	8.00	CREEK TO COAST	4.00	BLINKY BILL: (G)
		8.30	PROVIDENCE: "Pilot". A Beverly Hills plastic surgeon gives up her career to move back home and practice medicine. (PG)	4.30	ARTHUR: (G)
				5.00	CATDOG: (G)
				5.30	ALEX MACK
				6.00	HEARTBREAK HIGH
				6.30	MOTHER & SON: "Baby".
		10.30	MILLENNIUM: "Thirteen Years Later".	7.00	ABC NEWS
7.30	EMTV TOKSAVE			7.30	SEVEN-THIRTY REPORT
7.33	3RD TEST CRICKET	11.30	SEVEN NIGHTLY NEWS	8.00	DIVING SCHOOL: "Under Pressure". (G)
11.30	BENNY HINN MINISTRY: "This is Your Day".(Rpt)	12.00	INFORMERCIAL	8.30	THE BILL: "Shoot The Messenger/Too Little, Too Late". Boulton is missing after a surveillance operation goes wrong. An assault investigation is hampered by the reluctance of a witness to come forward.
		1.00	NBC TODAY		
		3.00	TELEMALL		
12.00	EMTV NEWS REPLAY	4.00	LAPD – LIFE ON THE BEAT		
12.30	***TEST PATTERN***	4.45	ZOO LIFE WITH JACK HANNA		
		5.10	VIDEO POWER	9.30	THE AUSTRALIAN SPORTS AWARDS 1999
		5.35	SAVED BY THE BELL		
				10.25	ABC NEWS - LATE EDITION
				10.30	MADSON (Rpt)

Source: *Post Courier*, Papua New Guinea, 29 November 1999, p.22

C O M M E N T _____

You have probably identified some of the values which are embodied in *Neighbours*, *Wheel of Fortune* or *The Bill*. And considering the relevance of such programmes to the Papua New Guinea context probably conjures up some bizarre juxtapositions. But it's the third question which is perhaps the most interesting and most problematic: how can we assess the *effects* of the media? Broadly speaking, media research has found no such direct effects, no measurable impact as common sense might suggest or popular accounts often assume. Rather, researchers have examined the meaning that television has for us in our daily lives. They have found that we don't passively or uncritically receive messages after these have been **encoded** in broadcast material. Rather, audiences are *active* in reading cultural texts. In a complex process they bring their own cultural predispositions and resources to bear in interpreting and making sense of television programmes. The outcome is far from straightforward or predictable, but a complex and varied picture with considerable diversity of both viewing behaviour and sense-making, as cultural goods are translated and adapted.

Encoding
The process whereby producers' *meanings* are represented or embodied in cultural texts.

_____

Obviously this is central to the cultural imperialism thesis. What sense *is* made of imported programming? To answer this question we need to examine consumption, to see how domination, negotiation or resistance occur. In this we shift from *quantitative* to *qualitative* research, from measuring in terms of pre-determined categories to focusing on meaning and interpretation.

The anthropologist Daniel Miller has examined the viewing of *The Young and the Restless* in Trinidad (Miller, 1992; also discussed in Miller, 1997). He rejects the notion that this US-produced soap works as a vehicle for exporting US and consumer culture. To the contrary, he found the programme 'localized' as Trinidadians made sense of it through the framework of local practices and understandings. It was a focus for gossip and scandal of a sexual nature, in a way which resonated with local concepts, understandings and situations:

> Typical comments would be: '... the same thing you see on the show will happen here, you see the wife blackmailing the husband or the other way around, I was telling my sister-in-law, Liana in the picture, just like some bacchanal woman'; 'I believe marriage should be 50-50 not 30-70 the woman have to be strong she have to believe in her vows no matter what ... that make me remember *The Young and the Restless*, Nicky wants her marriage to work but Victor is in love with somebody else, but she still holding on.'

> (Miller, 1997, p.29)

So it worked to reproduce local culture rather than to obliterate it in a process of homogenization. This is an example of the complex *interpenetration* of the global and the local referred to in Chapter 1, Section 3.1: the local becomes more globally integrated, though in the process does not lose its distinctiveness.

Another study has explored the varying significance of the view of one television series held by a range of social and national groups (Liebes and Katz, 1993). *Dallas* is a US soap opera which was transmitted in over a hundred countries in the 1980s, and is particularly interesting because it is seen by some as epitomizing the materialism which constitutes the core of what is so pernicious about US culture. Dallas became both 'a metaphor for the conquest of the world by an American television serial' and 'the most popular program in the world' (Liebes and Katz, 1993, p.5). Liebes and Katz explored the cross-cultural decodings of the series on three continents, and found evidence of different readings based on different cultural backgrounds. What they found was not any straightforward adoption by viewers of what might reasonably be seen as the dominant views of the series – notably the attractiveness of getting rich – but a series of widely divergent interpretations. Russians, for example, were critical of the politics of *Dallas*, and Arab groups were sensitive to what they saw as the dangers of Western culture and of Western moral degeneracy.

So the effects of television are more complex and diverse than suggested by simplistic notions of effects or of passive audiences. More than this, the strength and resilience of recipient, non-Western culture needs to be acknowledged. Rather than a passive process, we find that television is taken up and used in unpredicted and varied ways. Its viewers are not simply passive recipients of global culture, but are active, sense-making, agents.

SUMMARY

Transformationalists acknowledge important changes which are taking place in global culture flows, but see the outcome of these as more complex and less unidimensional than inter-nationalists or globalists suggest. By and large, they are critics of the cultural imperialism thesis.

- Cultural imperialism is a Western or US-centric story. International television flows do not simply demonstrate domination. Flows are regional as well as global, the flow is often not a measure of domination. Understanding the implications of television flows is complex.

- Ratings suggest that domestically produced programmes attract the highest audiences. Imports are often 'filler' for offpeak slots. Volume is not a measure of the significance of imported programming for national television.

- National cultural identity is a problematic notion. It is often used in undemocratic senses, and assumes that cultures are homogeneous, which is outdated in an era of multiculturalism and hybridity.

- Reading cultural texts is complex. Their significance cannot be assumed. Audiences bring their own cultural resources to bear in making sense of television programmes; and cultural readings are diverse.

5 CULTURE AND TECHNOLOGY

● ●

From the outset of this chapter I have been examining both culture and technology. Global culture is disseminated via an increasingly complex network of distribution technologies, and received by a growing plethora of domestic technologies. So technology is commonly implicated in debates about the burgeoning global dissemination of culture. As well as being prominent in debates about globalization, technology is seen by many as *the* defining characteristic of the contemporary era. Across the full breadth of social spheres and institutions – work, family, leisure, education and even the construction of identity – technological developments are seen as enormously significant for processes of transformation. According to this 'information society' thesis, information technology is the key feature of the contemporary social order, and information flows and networks lie at the heart of its organization.

You will have heard of 'the stone age', 'the steam age' and perhaps 'the computer age'. What do these expressions, which characterize particular historical epochs, have in common?

Implicit in such commonplace expressions is the notion that the technology – stone, steam or computers – is responsible for the dominant social characteristics of the era. The prevailing technology is seen as determining the form of social organization – hunter-gatherer society, the industrial revolution or 'the information society'. Technology is seen as the driving force of history. This is the argument of **technological determinism**. An example of technological determinism would be to argue that computers and telecommunications technologies *create* the information society.

One of the troubles with technological determinism is that, although technologies have 'effects', these are often not built in to the technology but are a result of how it is introduced. New technologies, for example, don't *have* to lead to redundancies when introduced to the workplace – but commonly they do. That they do so is because of the social arrangements governing the context of their introduction – a particular kind of market economy.

More than this, technological determinism ignores the fact that technologies are shaped by societies in the first place. The computer and today's communication technologies don't come from nowhere, nor are they simply the result of some abstract genius on the part of their inventors. Rather, they can be seen as a direct outcome of the Cold War and the research and development budget of, in particular, the US Department of Defense. Society,

Technological determinism
The commonplace assumption that societies are determined by their prevailing technologies.

in the form of the Cold War, shaped the technology – rather than the other way around. Had affluent societies determined other priorities in the post-war period, then we might well have seen the emergence of more sophisticated health or educational technologies – instead of technologies in health and education consisting in large part of applications of technologies which were designed for other, military, uses. So, whilst technological determinists focus on the social effects of technology, we can see that technologies are social in their origins as well as their effects – they are socially shaped.

Whilst there seems some logic to the argument that new technology is important for understanding late modernity, we need to be wary of technological determinism. Standage's account of the arrival of the telegraph shows us that it is not only today that new technologies have been greeted with excessive claims about their revolutionary significance and with arguments that their arrival heralds a new society. Histories of the arrival of the telegraph, the telephone, radio and television make pretty sobering (and fascinating) reading. Such histories show that, unlike the apocalyptic claims of Bill Gates and others, the change wreaked by technology is usually incremental and gradual. The impact of each of these communication technologies was not apparent until several decades after its arrival. So instead of an 'information revolution', maybe the Internet and other new information and communication technologies are best understood as a continuation of some long-running tendencies, rather than hearalding a profoundly new social order.

SUMMARY

- New technologies are key components of cultural globalization: they also lie at the core of 'information society' debates.

- Histories of the arrival of new technologies in earlier eras suggest that – although greeted as revolutionary – their impact is usually gradual.

- Rhetoric and discourse about new communication technologies tend to attribute to the technology considerable determining capacity. This is an example of technological determinism – the notion that technology is a fundamental determinant of key features of society.

- Sociologists, while recognizing that technologies constrain, point out that technologies are themselves shaped by the society that gave rise to them – they are 'socially shaped'.

6 CONCLUSION

● ●

We have seen that the world is becoming increasingly saturated with television and programming flows. Global media corporations are impinging – to varying degrees – on national broadcasting regimes, through digital, satellite and cable systems. The quantitative evidence on interconnection, however, is interpreted in a variety of ways.

Positive globalists extol the virtues of the 'global village', of instant, worldwide communication and the multiplicity of voices which can be heard. No longer are we subject to the paternalism and elitism of national broadcasting systems – which are having to respond to the global challenge with new forms of programming. Pessimistic globalists also examine structures, and focus on increasing inequalities and the unaccountable and growing power of the global media corporations. An important variant is Schiller's cultural imperialism thesis, which points to global cultural homogenization and sees this as operating in the interests of the USA and the West.

Inter-nationalists focus on the continuities for local, national, cultures. They point to the profound limits to global broadcasting, and the resilience of public service and national television. The national nature of the press and regulatory bodies supports the argument. The case of the telegraph cautions us that digital technologies and the Internet, in social terms, are perhaps not new.

The picture is more complex for transformationalists who focus on qualitative questions of meaning: the sense that is made of imported television, and its relationship to indigenous culture. What we find is that flows are more complex than suggested by the globalizers; but – crucially – that local cultures and differences remain, despite the global flows. National cultures remain resilient and distinctive despite MTV, CNN and Hollywood.

In Section 5 we looked briefly at what some claim is driving these changes – the 'information technology revolution'. Technologies, however, arise from cultures – which is not to deny that, once they have arrived, they have effects.

We have examined various perspectives for making sense of the processes, flows and patterns of cultural globalization. Many focus on *structures* – of global corporations, of culture flows, of cultural domination: these perspectives commonly use *quantitative* evidence. Other perspectives, which tend to use *qualitative* approaches, are more concerned with *agency* – on the part of individual nations and communities, and of individuals: these explore the sense-making which is implicated in the consumption of cultural texts, and the *active* nature of audiences. All would acknowledge that cultural space and cultural systems are more contested than ever before, and that the diversity of cultural products and technologies are developing and circulating at ever-increasing rates – which makes it hard to keep track of the picture. The ever-shifting array of global corporations are vying with one another for market share, while nation-states are retreating in the face of this onslaught, fuelled as it is by the spread of liberal economic ideas. The future is uncertain, dependent on a combination of these media corporations, nation-states, technological developments and, crucially, the preferences of consumers in their everyday lives.

REFERENCES

Allen, J. (2004) 'Power: its institutional guises (and disguises)' in Hughes, G. and Fergusson, R. (eds) *Ordering Lives: Family, Work and Welfare* (2nd edn), London, Routledge/The Open University.

Barker, C. (1997) *Global Television: An Introduction*, Blackwell, Oxford.

Cantor, M. and Cantor, J. (1992) *Prime Time Television: Content and Control*, London, Sage.

Collins, R. (1990) *Culture, Communication and National Identity: The Case of Canadian Television*, Toronto, University of Toronto Press.

Dorfman, A. and Mattelart, A. (1975) *How to Read Donald Duck: Imperialist Ideology in the Disney Comic*, International General, New York.

Dyson, K. and Humphreys, J. (eds) (1990) *Political Economy of Communications*, London, Routledge.

Hannerz, U. (1990) 'Cosmopolitans and locals in world culture', *Theory, Culture and Society*, vol.7, nos2–3, pp.237–51.

Hebdige, D. (1988) *Hiding in the Light*, London, Routledge.

Herman, E. and McChesney, R. (1997) *The Global Media: The New Missionaries of Corporate Capitalism*, London, Cassell.

Home Office (1986) *Financing the BBC*, Report of the Committee on Financing the BBC (Chair: Professor A. Peacock), London, HMSO.

ITC (Independent Television Commission) (1997) 'Estimated audience share figures for selected television channels received in British Islands in the 12 months ended 31 December 1996', press release, February.

Liebes, T. and Katz, E. (1993) *The Export of Meaning: Cross-Cultural Readings of Dallas* (2nd edn), Cambridge, Polity.

Masmoudi, M. (1979) 'The new world information order', *Journal of Communication*, vol.29, no.2, pp.172–85.

Mattelart, A., Delacourt, X. and Mattelart, M. (1984) *International Image Markets*, London, Comedia.

McBride, S. (1980) *Many Voices, One World*, Paris, UNESCO.

Miller, D. (1992) 'The young and the restless in Trinidad: a case of the local and the global in mass consumption' in Silverstone, R. and Hirsch, E. (eds) *Consuming Technology*, London, Routledge.

Miller, D. (1997) 'Consumption and its consequences' in Mackay, H. (ed.) *Consumption and Everyday Life*, London, Sage/The Open University.

O'Regan (1992) 'New and declining audiences: contemporary transformations on Hollywood's international market' in Jacka, E. (ed.) *Continental Shift*, Sydney, Local Consumption Publications.

Phillips, W. (1997) 'Broadcast/Barb Top 70: week ending 29 June 1997', *Broadcast*, 18 July, pp.30–1.

Rheingold, H. (1995) *The Virtual Community*, London, Mandarin Paperbacks.

Schiller, H. (1991) 'Not yet the post-imperialist era', *Critical Studies in Mass Communication*, vol.8, pp.13–28.

Screen Digest, London, Screen Digest Ltd (monthly).

Sinclair, J., Jacka, E. and Cunningham, S. (1996) 'Peripheral vision' in Sinclair, J., Jacka, E. and Cunningham S. (eds) *New Patterns in Global Television: Peripheral Vision*, Oxford, Oxford University Press.

Smith, A.D. (1995) *Nations and Nationalism in a Global Era*, Oxford, Polity.

Sparks, C. (1998) 'Is there a global public sphere?' in Thussu, D.K. (ed.) *Electronic Empires: Global Media and Local Resistance*, London, Arnold.

Standage, T. (1998) *The Victorian Internet*, London, Wiedenfeld & Nicolson.

Therborn, G. (1995) *European Modernity and Beyond: The Trajectory of European Societies 1945–2000*, London, Sage.

Thussu, D.K. (1998) 'Introduction' in Thussu, D.K. (ed.) *Electronic Empires. Global Media and Local Resistance*, London. Arnold.

Tomlinson, J. (1997) 'Internationalism, globalization and cultural imperialism' in Thompson, K. (ed.) *Media and Cultural Regulation*, London, Sage.

UNESCO (1986) *International Flows of Selected Cultural Goods*, Statistical Reports and Studies, No. 28, Paris Division of Statistics on Culture and Communication, Office of Statistics, UNESCO.

UNESCO (1989) *World Communication Report*, Paris, United Nations Educational, Scientific and Cultural Organization.

UNESCO (1994) *Statistical Yearbook, 1994*, Paris, United Nations Educational, Scientific and Cultural Organization.

UNESCO (1998) *Statistical Yearbook, 1998*, United Nations Educational, Scientific and Cultural Organization, Paris, and Bernan Press, Lanham, MD, USA.

UNESCO (1999) *Statistical Yearbook, 1999*, Paris, United Nations Educational, Scientific and Cultural Organization.

Varis, T. (1984) 'The international flow of television programmes', *Journal of Communication*, vol.34, no.1, pp.143–52.

Varis, T. (1985) *International Flow of Television Programmes*, Reports and Papers on Mass Communication, No.100, Paris, UNESCO.

FURTHER READING

For an accessible text which rehearses the range of debates and evidence regarding global television, addressing both industries and culture, see Chris Barker (1997) *Global Television. An Introduction*, Oxford, Blackwell.

For an account of patterns of media ownership, see Edward Herman and Robert McChesney (1997) *The Global Media: The New Missionaries of Corporate Capitalism*, London, Cassell. Herman and McChesney examine in detail the interests, activities and strategies of the global media corporations.

For an introduction and evaluation of debates about cultural domination, see John Tomlinson (1991) *Cultural Imperialism*, London, Pinter. He examines the assumptions which underlie the various positions on the spread of global cultural commodities.

For a review of debates about broadcasting audiences, see Shaun Moores (1993) *Interpreting Audiences: The Ethnography of Media Consumption*, London, Sage. Moores introduces and examines the breadth of approaches for making sense of how viewers interact with television texts.

On approaches to understanding the social shaping of technology, see Donald MacKenzie and Judy Wajcman (eds) (1999) *The Social Shaping of Technology* (2nd edn), Buckingham, Open University Press. This edited collection includes a range of fascinating case studies.

Economic globalization?

Bob Kelly and Raia Prokhovnik

1 INTRODUCTION

● ●

It is now almost impossible to pick up a newspaper or listen to the news without either being confronted by the word 'globalization' or being faced with issues relating to its economic impact. For instance, financial scandals or crises are said to be having ripple effects throughout the world, or jobs are being gained or lost through the business decisions and activities of large corporations. The quotes that follow give you some flavour of the ways such developments are being interpreted.

> 'Globalization' is the process of corporate structuring that focuses a company's core competency on a single worldwide market, creating growth and profit opportunities [...] It affects employees, customers, and suppliers. The fundamental precepts of the vision are free flow of commerce, labor and capital, and belief in the ability of an individual to significantly and favorably impact larger social and economic systems.
>
> (The Quadral Group of worldwide business advisors, 1996, p.1)

> The ideologies and rules of economic globalization [...] have destroyed the livelihoods of millions of people, often leaving them homeless, landless and hungry, while removing their access to even the most basic public services such as health and medical care, education, sanitation, fresh water, public transport, job training and the like. The record shows that economic globalization makes things worse for the poor, not better [...]
>
> (Mander and Barker, 2002, p.2)

> states are by no means powerless in the face of economic globalization [...] After all, governments and central banks continue to exert major influence on money supplies and interest rates [...] Recent years have seen increased intergovernmental consultations to obtain tighter official oversight of offshore finance.
>
> (Scholte, 2001, p.536)

> trade linkages among Canadian provinces [...] are many times more extensive than those between the provinces and American states that are just as close as the snowy owl flies: Toronto trades more than ten times as much with Vancouver as with Seattle. The same holds true between the industrial core and the developing periphery. National borders today are still tall barriers to movement of goods, capital and most of all labor.
>
> (DeLong, 1999, p.6)

although transborder manufacturing through global factories has affected a significant proportion of certain industries, it has involved but a small percentage of overall world production. Most processes have remained contained within one country [...]

(Scholte, 2001, p.535)

These quotes offer contrasting pictures of the extent and significance of economic globalization. The first two indicate a basic division between those who see great opportunities for increased trade, investment and growth and those who predict or fear the impoverishment and exploitation of large sections of the world's population. The third and fourth extracts consider that states and national economies are still important. The fifth quote suggests that there is a great deal of hype about economic globalization, in terms of both present impact and inevitability.

On 3 July 2002 *The Guardian* announced in its financial news that 'Jensen takes road out of Britain'. The story then focused on a number of examples of British companies that had recently decided or were considering the withdrawal of production from Britain and relocation to other parts of the world. Jensen, the producer of the SV8 car, was announcing the possibility of transferring its production from its plant in Speke, Merseyside to a 'lower-cost' country such as South Africa. The plant had only been re-established as a production unit in 1998 after receiving financial support from Liverpool city council and Merseyside Special Investment Fund.

A number of similar stories appeared during the same year. As *The Guardian* points out, in February, Royal Doulton announced the closure of its ceramics plant in Staffordshire, with its intention to move to Indonesia. In May, Raleigh declared its intention to stop bicycle production in Nottingham and transfer to factories in East Asia.

What are we to make of these moves in some of the UK's most prestigious and traditional industries? Do such economic shifts warrant the term globalization to explain them, or can they be absorbed into a more traditional economic understanding?

This chapter, then, explores the debate over the idea of 'economic globalization'. Is it a new and inevitable process? Should we accept and welcome it, or should we be joining anti-globalization protestors who take to the streets of cities in which world economic leaders meet, on the grounds that there are serious losers as well as winners from these changes? Should we focus on trying to harness benefits from it? Or should we be sceptical about the extent of the changes?

Each of the three core chapters of this book, on cultural, economic and political globalization, has the task of highlighting one of the three major interpretations. This chapter aims to highlight the *inter-nationalist* case. The inter-nationalist interpretation seeks to present a coherent view of international economics but one that rejects the concept of radical change. The inter-nationalist case disputes the very use of the term economic globalization. It seeks to contest what it sees as over-inflated claims made especially by the globalists, in both their 'positive' and 'pessimistic' guises. The inter-nationalist position also contests the transformationalist perspective on the grounds that its attempt to sound reasonable by taking the middle ground is misconceived. For these reasons, and to enable you to have plenty of material with which to make comparisons and evaluate the inter-nationalist case, it is important to start the chapter with an outline of the globalist and transformationalist positions on economic globalization. The chapter then focuses on the theoretical criticisms, empirical evidence, and alternative arguments offered by the inter-nationalists.

2 APPROACHING THE DEBATE ON ECONOMIC GLOBALIZATION

From what you have read so far you will have realized that the notion of *globalization* is subject to a range of different definitions and interpretations. Some stress the development of a common global culture. Others debate whether the political power of the nation-state to deal with the wide range of challenges it faces is declining; these challenges include the international drugs trade, the power of large international companies, the increasing influence of the USA over economic and political matters, and the desperation of would-be 'economic' migrants. Some suggest great opportunities and benefits for the world's population at large, others see perils and impoverishment for many individuals, groups and societies. Some analyses see globalization as a sudden and rapid reaction to changes in communications and information technology, while other interpretations see it as a continuation and perhaps acceleration of a centuries-old trend. Some think the notion is overrated and the term redundant. At its most radical the concept suggests a complete metamorphosis of the way in which people identify themselves and live their lives. At the very least it suggests a whole set of new opportunities and challenges for people and institutions to negotiate.

There is general agreement, however, that international trade and some forms of investment have been increasing in recent decades, but also that at present there is not a single global economy that totally controls the production and consumption patterns of every human being. What we have, therefore, is not a clear-cut division of views between extreme positions, but a continuum on which the views of particular writers can be placed in relation to each other, as shown on Figure 3.1.

FIGURE 3.1   The 'debate on economic globalization' continuum

These terms and their location on 'the globalization continuum' are used by us to mark conflicting strands in the analysis of contemporary events. The actual contribution to the debate and particular position of any given author may be more complex. Debates on globalization are complex and wide-ranging, but we hope that the modelling of them under the three sub-headings (with the additional sub-division of the globalists into positive and pessimistic) will sharpen up the differences and help to make these debates more accessible.

A C T I V I T Y 3.1

Now that you have been introduced to the 'globalist', 'transformationalist' and 'inter-nationalist' positions on economic globalization, have another look at the five quotes that started this chapter. See if you can identify which quote expresses which position.

C O M M E N T

The first quote relates to the positive globalist position, and the second one to the pessimistic globalist perspective. The third extract reflects the transformationalist viewpoint, while the fourth could be used by both the transformationalist and inter-nationalist cases. The final quote reflects the inter-nationalist perspective.

While this chapter focuses on economic matters, it is clear that they shape and are shaped by cultural and political affairs. As we proceed, do bear in mind the ways in which the cultural, the political and the economic interrelate and are interdependent in the international sphere. Within a state, cultural traditions and values influence the way politicians, business people, workers and consumers think and behave, while political authorities lay down the legal and regulatory framework in which business transactions are conducted. As we shall see, feminist writers develop some of these points, arguing that the scope of economic globalization has been defined too narrowly. Conversely, debates about *economic* globalization are fundamental to questions about cultural and political globalization. At an individual level, economic matters and economic differences help structure our identities and position in society, while at an international level, trading strength and investment power are important in establishing political power. If American or any other culture is seen to be dominating the world, it is partly because the investments and products of McDonald's, Microsoft, Disney, etc. are so visible and significant in other parts of the globe. Concern about the loss of political sovereignty and the ability of states to act independently arises from fear of the power of multinational corporations and international economic organizations such as the World Trade Organization (WTO), as well as from fear of the power of other states. As we shall see, the globalist, transformationalist, and inter-nationalist positions each interpret differently the relationship between economic matters on the one hand and political and cultural affairs on the other.

3 THE GLOBALIST PERSPECTIVE ON ECONOMIC GLOBALIZATION

●   ●

International trade

International trade (the combination of imports and exports) is best measured in terms of what proportion of the total merchandise output (manufacturing, mining, agricultural and, increasingly, service industries) it accounts for. What matters for international trade is the level relative to total output. If the remainder consumed within countries of origin is low, then the level of international trade is more significant.

Globalization [... is] the process by which markets and production in different countries are becoming increasingly interdependent due to the dynamics of trade in goods and services and flows of capital and technology.

(European Commission, 1997, p.45)

'Globalization' has a frenetic pace and is a dramatic force of worldwide supply and demand. Companies that adjust to its speed discover the force of change greatly in their favor. Those that cannot adjust find they cannot escape or avoid the competitive forces created by this process.

(The Quadral Group, 1996, p.1)

Economic globalists understand globalization as a phenomenon concerning the growing integration of the national economies of most states in the world, based on five interrelated drivers of change:

● growing **international trade** resulting from lower trade barriers and more competition

- increasing financial flows in such forms as **foreign direct investment (FDI)** and technology transfers; FDI can take the form of 'greenfield' or brand new investment or 'mergers with and acquisitions of' existing enterprises, and this is but one of the forms of capital flow which take place
- increased communications via both the Internet and 'traditional' media
- technological advances in electronics, transportation, bioengineering, etc.
- increased labour mobility.

Foreign direct investment (FDI)

A major form of borrowing and lending in the international economy, undertaken by and helping to define multinational corporations (MNCs). When an MNC sets up economic activity abroad under its direct control, it effectively lends to the country in which it is investing, and that country therefore borrows from the MNC's home country.

ACTIVITY 3.2

FIGURE 3.2 Long term trends of world merchandise trade and output, by volume, 1950–2001 (volume indices: 1990 = 100)
Source: WTO, 2002

Describe what the graph in Figure 3.2 shows about the growth of merchandising trade, relative to the lines for merchandising output and world gross domestic product (GDP).

C O M M E N T

The graph indicates that, while all three measures have risen, the growth in merchandising trade has increased most, particularly in the years since 1990, far outstripping the growth of world GDP and merchandising output. Note that this is a line graph that is based on index figures; that is, it shows how total units of output have changed over time compared with a base year – it does not show total units of output, trade, etc.

According to the globalist interpretation, the outcome of growing integration is that a single worldwide economy is emerging and functioning. Globalists consider that in the single global economy in the making, economic processes are increasingly 'stretched' so that events and decisions taken in a particular state or region have a significant impact in other distant parts of the world. It has been suggested, for instance, that the 1997/98 East Asian financial crisis, which resulted in widespread bankruptcies in countries such as Thailand, Malaysia and Korea, and consequent devaluation of shares in Europe and North America, was originally caused by the decisions of a small number of financial traders in New York (DeLong, 1999, p.1). Certainly the threat of economic disruption in one continent can have an immediate impact on share prices and economic transactions in others.

Multinational corporation (MNC)
A multinational corporation is any company which has some of its productive capacity located in a number of states, either as a result of new foreign direct investment (FDI) in new production facilities or through the acquisition of shares in already existing foreign companies.

Associated with this, they argue, there has been an 'intensification' of flows and networks of economic interaction, with communication systems spreading throughout the world and negating the significance of physical distance. Developments in information technology are seen as central here, enabling the co-ordination of operations of **multinational corporations (MNCs)** and their subsidiaries and independent suppliers across international borders and oceans. Individuals and enterprises can now use the Internet to buy products of their choice without moving from their homes and offices, with the potential of avoiding the scrutiny, restrictions, and perhaps even the tax-raising powers of the state.

It is further suggested that there is an increasing interpenetration of economies, with the products of very different states appearing side-by-side in localities across the globe. In towns and cities we are commonly faced with competition to supply our evening meal from Indian, Chinese, Greek, Italian, American, etc. cuisine of varying degrees of authenticity and hybridity. Multinational companies such as Unilever, Proctor and Gamble, Nestlé, and Sony seem to dominate advertising hoardings and outlets for their particular products throughout the world. International investment means that any firm which appears as a household name may well be part of some foreign or internationally-owned conglomerate. We may, for example, think of products such as 'Ariel' and 'Daz' as typically British, and yet they are actually made by the US-based MNC, Procter and Gamble.

At the same time there has been a growth in the 'global infrastructure' to regulate and control the developments that are taking place. At one level this takes the form of information and communications technology based in a few cities such as Frankfurt and London where major financial decision making takes place. At another, there are formal organizations such as the International Monetary Fund (IMF) and the World Trade Organization (WTO) which make policies and rules that structure the way all states and businesses, to a greater or lesser extent, operate.

3.1   The evidence used by economic globalists

> Spurred by robust economic growth, global integration deepened substantially in 2000, a year that saw record gains in most indicators of international exchange. The value of world merchandise exports, for instance, surged by more than 12% in 2000, while trade in services jumped by 6.1% – both more than triple the previous year's growth rate.
>
> (American Foreign Policy Association, 2002, p.3)

In support of the globalist thesis, some economists have suggested that since the 1970s trading and investment relationships have developed in ways that indicate much more intense cross-national integration than there has ever been in the past. They cite dramatic improvements at a global level in transport technology, advances in communications and computing technology, and the know-how to make use of these developments as the background factors which have led to dramatic changes in international trade. Now a larger proportion of the manufactured goods, mining products and agricultural goods of the major industrialized countries such as the USA, France and Germany is exported than was ever the case in the past (Grieco and Ikenberry, 2002, p.3).

Another form of evidence used to underpin the idea of a global economy is the amount of trade taking place in the form of the transfer of goods at various stages of production, so particular products are the result of productive contributions from various states in the world. For example, Grieco and Ikenberry (2002, p.3) quote an estimate that by the late 1990s 'about 60% of the value of the hardware of personal computers consisted of imported components'. As part of this development, several fast-growing newly industrializing countries, such as South Korea and China, are now major exporters of intermediate and finished manufacturing goods to the so-called 'developed' countries. Such countries were the source of 22 per cent of all manufactured goods imported by the USA in the late 1990s, up from about 10 per cent in the early 1970s.

In addition to trade expansion, all forms of foreign investment (i.e. the financing of investment projects as opposed to dealing in bonds and shares) have increased greatly, with a particular emphasis on foreign direct investment. It has been estimated that the value of such US investment was equal to 20 per cent of US GNP in the mid 1990s as against about 7 per cent in 1960.

Prior to the attacks on Washington and New York in September 2001, the world tourist industry was rapidly growing with an estimated 698.9 million international arrivals in 2000, compared with 457.2 million a decade previously. Similarly, international communications have continued to grow, with an estimated increase of cross-border telephone traffic of roughly 10 billion minutes in 2000. In the same year, the number of Internet-linked computers rose by 44 per cent and 80 million users logged on to the Internet for the first time (American Foreign Policy Association, 2002, p.3).

If we take changes in world merchandise trade by major product group (Figure 3.3), we can see how patterns have varied but have, nevertheless, recorded significant increases in the period between 1950 and 1999.

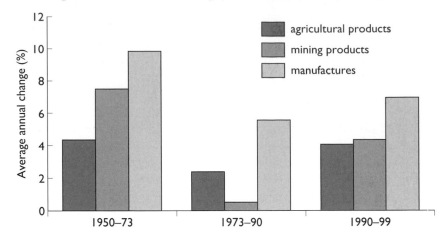

FIGURE 3.3   Average annual change in trade in agricultural, mining and manufactured products, 1950–99
Source: WTO, 2000

ACTIVITY 3.3

Look at the bar chart in Figure 3.3. What are the key points being displayed?

C O M M E N T _____

- In each period there is an average annual increase for each product group
- The increase in trade in manufactured goods is consistently higher than for the other categories
- The rate of increase for each product group was lowest in the 1973–90 period and was greatest in the 1950–73 period
- The general conclusion from this evidence would be that world trade has greatly increased over the last three decades but that the rate of growth is irregular.

3.2 Winners and losers: we are all potential winners from economic globalization

Consumers are its [globalization's] principal beneficiary. Its benefits in terms of faster growth, quicker access to new technology, cheaper imports and greater competition are available for all. Globalization has made the world economy more efficient and has created hundreds of millions of jobs, mainly, but not only, in developing countries.

(International Chamber of Commerce, 2000)

It is the most recent period of globalisation, from 1980, which has seen a radical shift in the fortune of many of the world's poor. For the first time, there has been a sustained fall in the number of people living in poverty – defined as people living on less than $1 a day.

(*The Economist*, 5 December 2001)

Positive globalists see a range of important benefits for all countries and peoples in the processes that have been taking place. **Economic liberals** (those that advocate a free economic market through deregulation of controls by governments) generally believe that globalization is a positive trend that inevitably benefits consumers by increasing the efficiency of markets. Thomas Friedman claims that the era of globalization is one of peace, exemplified by the fact that no two countries that have allowed McDonald's restaurants to be established have subsequently gone to war! (Friedman, 1999, p.197.)

According to this version of the globalist perspective particular benefits accrue to the poorer countries. It is suggested that an integrated global market accelerates the transfer of technology from the richer to the poorer countries. Moreover, the richer countries have a surplus of funds to lend, and this provides a real opportunity for rapid industrialization of poorer

Economic liberals
Liberalism is a set of beliefs that gives priority to individuals to make choices. Economic liberals believe that individual freedom is best promoted by increasing the role of the 'free' market in both social and economic policy areas. They are keen to limit the scope of government intervention in and regulation of the market, and are prepared to tolerate wide inequalities as a result.

FIGURE 3.4   Japanese and Chinese car companies clinch joint venture

countries. It is also argued that removing trade barriers in turn reduces the role of governments, and therefore attacks the problems of corruption, stagnation and bureaucratic barriers to growth which have beset the poorer countries in the past (DeLong, 1999, p.5).

The American Foreign Policy Association and a management consulting firm A.T. Kearney have put together a set of indicators which support the positive globalist position. The figures for 1998–2000 suggest that the world's most globalized countries boast greater income equality than their less globalized counterparts. In addition, rather than globalization reflecting US or superpower dominance, it was found that the most globalized economies tend to be those of small nations for which openness accesses goods, services and capital that would not otherwise be available. Singapore ranked as the world's most global nation in 1998, with the USA only in twelfth place, while in 2000 Ireland topped the list. Global integration continues to grow, with the value of world merchandise exports increasing by more than 12 per cent in 2000 and trade in services by 6.1 per cent. The indicators span 'information technology, finance, trade, politics, travel and personal communication to evaluate levels of global integration in dozens of advanced economies and key emerging markets worldwide' (American Foreign Policy Association, 2002, p.2).

3.3 Winners and losers: we are all potential losers from economic globalization

> politicians like Democratic congressman David Bonior begin speeches by noting three things that come to the US from Mexico – dirty trucks, drugs, and hepatitis.

(DeLong, 1999, p.1)

> A report by the United Nations […] found that inequalities between rich and poor within countries, and among countries, are quickly expanding, and that the global trading and finance system is one of the primary causes.

(Mander and Barker, 2002, p.1)

These quotes point to the problems highlighted by pessimistic globalists; namely that open borders and deregulated trading arrangements can present problems for rich as well as poor countries. In both rich and poor countries, some people may be becoming extremely rich, but the widening inequalities can cause longer-term problems of poverty, resentment, social exclusion and political unrest. Pessimistic globalizers also argue that the impact of globalization in undermining borders is seen in the example of reprocessing imported nuclear waste, and in the use of the Internet in reducing state powers to control the economy and organize taxation. It also increases the legal authority of non-governmental organizations such as the

World Trade Organization to 'override local and national authority if there is a violation of the terms of the agreement' and so to 'discipline sovereign states' (Sassen, 1998, p.98). The view that we are all losers is strengthened by the argument that 'contemporary patterns of economic globalization have shifted power away from democratically elected governments towards unaccountable global market forces'. The argument is that since 'capital is increasingly mobile, significant constraints are created on the power of national governments to pursue progressive economic policies or redistributive social policies'. Thus, it 'is not that all capital is necessarily "footloose", but it is the fact that capital and plant could be moved to alternative investment opportunities that creates strong pressures to market appeasing and supporting policies' (Held and McGrew, 2000, p.250).

The former World Bank Chief Economist Joseph Stiglitz has been quoted as saying that the 'borderless world through which goods and services flow is also a borderless world through which other things can flow that are less positive' (American Foreign Policy Association, 2002, p.1). By this he meant that organized crime and terrorist networks can make effective use of global communications and technology. Similarly, the 'shrinking' of the world can also facilitate global pollution. Spillage from damaged oil tankers is regularly reported as a threat to both wildlife and human livelihood in many parts of the world, and following outbreaks of various diseases among livestock, major concerns have been raised about the dangers of trade in contaminated meat products.

A number of writers have pointed to the growing gaps between the rich and the poor that have occurred during the 'era of globalization' which can then

FIGURE 3.5 The global spread of drugs: a Colombian soldier guards confiscated cocaine with a value of US$120 million near the border with Ecuador

Median income
This is the income of
the person placed in the
middle of income
rankings. In a village of
101 people this would
be the income of the
51st highest earner.

threaten the political stability of those societies. In 1980 the **median income** in
the richest 10 per cent of countries was 77 times greater than that in the
poorest 10 per cent. By 1999 this difference had grown to 122 times (Weller *et
al.*, 2002, p.1). It has also been estimated by a radical pressure group in 1996
that the income of the world's then 358 billionaires was equal to the total
income of the poorest 45 per cent of the world's population (*Rally
Comrades!*, 1997, p.7). Pessimistic globalists also argue that within the richer
countries globalization leads to more import competition and the increasing
use of threats to move production to lower-wage localities, thereby
depressing wage rates while the incomes of managers rise. A World Bank
report in 2001 concluded that 'almost all industrial economies experienced
some increase in wage inequality among prime-aged males' (World Bank,
2001).

We can see how arguments about economic globalization quickly become
enmeshed with those about the political and cultural dimensions. Pessimistic
globalists hold that trade in cultural products threatens the language, culture
and identity of many peoples throughout the world. Similarly, individuals and
communities can be threatened by growing uncertainty, with the spread of
financial crises from one country to another. The most obvious example of
this took place in 1997–99 when the devaluation of the currency of Thailand
was followed by the collapse of currencies and stock markets in Indonesia,
Malaysia, South Korea, Japan and then Russia and South America. Investment
losses in Asia and Russia necessitated reduced lending to Brazil and the
Brazilian government in 1999 was forced to announce an austerity
programme and the official devaluation of the Brazilian currency, the *real*,
even though its own economic policies had generally been regarded as
reasonably prudent (Galbraith, 1999, p.2).

3.4 Winners and losers: those who lose most from economic globalization

> Why is a globalised economy good? Or, rather the question ought to be, for
> whom is it good? Statistics about the growing gap between the world's richest and
> poorest fifths are well known; the gap constantly widens [...] Opponents of
> globalisation are not wrong to protest, demonstrate or strike, for whatever else
> it does globalisation is bringing few benefits to the world's poorest nations.
>
> (Arnold, 2002, pp.24–5)

Pessimistic globalists can come from many different ideological positions, with
conservatives such as the American evangelist Pat Buchanan seeing it as a
conspiracy of international bankers against the American people, and
environmentalists such as Ralph Nader seeing it as the cause of pesticide-
laden fruit (DeLong, 1999, p.1). We saw that supporters of the view that
globalization offers potential benefits to all participants in the global economy

can often be located within economic liberalism. Many of those focusing on the groups who lose out are found within a **socialist or Marxist framework** which regards global capitalism as based on exploitation. Michael Albert, for example, argues that when trade takes place between a large multinational company and a local entity in a poorer country, 'the benefits do not go more to the weaker party with fewer assets, nor are they divided equally, but they go disproportionately to the stronger traders who thereby increase their relative dominance'. Albert contends that 'capitalist globalizers try to disempower the poor and already weak and to further empower the rich and already strong. The result: of the 100 largest economies in the world, 52 aren't countries; they are corporations' (Albert, 2001, p.1).

In *The Crisis of Globalization*, J.K. Galbraith puts the case very simply: 'The push of competition, deregulation, privatization and open capital markets has actually undermined economic prospects for many millions of the world's poorest people' (Galbraith, 1999, p.1). According to this view, inequalities between rich and poor, both within and between countries, are expanding. It is estimated that between 1988 and 1993 the share of the world's income going to the poorest 10 per cent of the world's population fell by over a quarter, whereas the share of the richest 10 per cent rose by 8 per cent (Mander and Barker, 2002, p.2). A Pakistani-based research centre report concludes that 'during the globalization phase about half-a-billion people in South Asia have experienced a decline in their incomes', with benefits accruing only 'to a small minority of educated urban population' (*The Times of India*, 2002, p.1). The perspective which highlights groups of those who lose most from globalization is summed up by a letter to *The Guardian*. It contends that globalization:

> has benefits and costs, and these are very unevenly distributed across the world. With more than a billion people living below a dollar a day and half the world living on less than two dollars, it's hard to argue that the current pattern of globalization is working well for the world's poor.
>
> (*The Guardian*, 11 October 2002)

Another powerful voice identifying a group who lose out from economic globalization competition is found in feminist writers. Feminist writers list various ways in which, for large groups of women, subordinate roles and lesser power in gender relations reinforces or worsens their existing invisibility and unequal treatment. Jill Steans notes that as 'the least unionized and poorest paid of all workers, women have been particularly vulnerable to the market policies which have continued to characterize global economic restructuring in the 1990s' (Steans, 2000, p.368). Saskia Sassen identifies three areas of the international economy where women's roles, especially with the 'expanded incorporation of Third World women into wage labour' (Sassen, 1998, p.130), go unrecognized or where their inequality is reinforced. In the first place, she argues, internationalized export-oriented commercial cash crop agriculture depends upon women, through their subsistence farming and household production, subsidizing the waged labour of men.

Socialist and Marxist frameworks
In contrast with economic liberals, socialists and Marxists see a continued conflict between the interests of an exploitative capital-owning class and the interests of the poor, disadvantaged and vulnerable in a society. They highlight the importance of collective and structural reforms over individual choices for bringing about greater social and economic equality.

FIGURE 3.6   The uneven distribution of costs and benefits of globalization

The second area, Sassen contends, is offshore internationalized manufacturing production. Under pressure from low-cost imports, a high proportion of lower-paid women makes up the workforce in poorer countries, drawn largely from women who had previously largely remained outside the industrial economy. Indeed, the evidence shows that export manufacturing has drawn new sections of the population into the labour force, most notably young women who, under conditions of more gradual industrialization, would not have entered the labour market in so massive and sudden a way. This development has also disrupted the unwaged work structures in communities of origin. Young men are left without partners, the households are left without the important contributions women make. Steans confirms the development of 'women ghettoized in assembly-line work with poor pay and prospects', as part of the general feminization of the workforce in both the North and the South (Steans, 2000, p.367). Sassen refers to such women workers in the South as an 'offshore proletariat' (Sassen, 1998, p.86), an 'invisible and disempowered class of workers' (Sassen, 1998, p.91) for whom work is simply a dead-end drudgery. Steans also observes that women's efforts to translate their paid employment into financial independence often come to nothing. This is due to their poor education and training, their burden of family responsibilities, and their lack of access to capital. More generally, the small number of firms with superprofit-making capacities in the globalized context of economic activity leads to a sharp polarization of profitability across and between sectors, increasing vulnerability for medium-sized companies. This situation also engenders a sharp distortion in the way that housing markets and labour markets operate, resulting in an increase of unregulated and exploitative informal labour, as well as 'the weakening role of the firm in structuring the employment relation', and 'the shift of labour market functions to the household' (Sassen, 1998, p.90).

The third area Sassen identifies is new patterns of migration, especially from rural to new urban labour-intensive industrial zones, as well as long-distance and regional migration. Migrations are stimulated by economic globalization. Sassen argues that migration patterns 'do not just happen: they are one outcome [...] in a more general dynamic of change' at a macro level (Sassen, 1998, p.116). Migration has specific negative effects for women by channelling women into subservient roles as well as into prostitution, and by dislocating family groups. Sassen notes that female migrants face 'a double disadvantage, one of sex and one of class', in terms of remuneration, opportunity, the kind of jobs they are channelled into, additional domestic responsibilities, and status (Sassen, 1998, p.115). The growth of new cities to meet the demands of economic globalization renders women workers and immigrants invisible, creating 'employment-centred urban poverty and marginality' (Sassen, 1998, p.88). She also notes that in service industries, dominated by financial companies, 'a large share of the jobs involved are low pay and manual, many held by women and immigrants'. Such work is 'never represented as part of the global economy', but is 'in fact part of the infrastructure of jobs involved in running and implementing the global economic system'.

Avtar Brah, Mary Hickman and Mairtin Mac an Ghaill also argue that the discussion of economic globalization needs to include migration and, in particular, the gendered effects of new and intensified migration patterns stimulated by globalization. If economic globalization is about the movement of capital and commodities, it is also about the movement of people. Migrants, minority ethnic groups, refugees and asylum-seekers are all seen as problems for the nation-state. Brah *et al.* note that 'a world market in labour does not exist in the same way as it does for goods and services. Labour markets are predominantly regulated at the national level, and multiple barriers are experienced by both "legal" and "illegal" migrants' (Brah *et al.*, 1999, p.5). In general, prospective migrants are far less likely to succeed than they were in the nineteenth century. The two exceptions are the 'club-class' migrant, 'predominantly male and most likely to be white – with high-level professional or managerial qualifications and technical skills, employed within the "core" sectors of the world economy', and 'women willing to travel in response to an increasing demand for domestic labour in middle-class or wealthy homes, or, in other low-paid sectors of the labour market'. While a free market policy and trade barriers can go hand in hand, Brah *et al.* argue that economic globalization is marked by a contradiction. They contend that the 'continuing need of the capitalist world economy for cheap labour in "secondary" sectors', does not sit comfortably with demands in First World countries to curtail so-called 'economic migrants' (Brah *et al.*, 1999, p.6).

Sassen's aim is to demonstrate that the common picture of the global economic system has been too narrow, underestimating the human costs involved. She remarks, for instance, that the visible face of a corporation (buildings, managers in suits) is far easier to 'see' in an advanced economic system 'than are truckers and other industrial service workers, even though these are necessary ingredients'. Moreover what is 'seen' and what is invisible relates closely to who is valued in the system and who is not. In addition Sassen argues that much of what we still think of in terms of immigration and ethnicity 'is actually a series of processes having to do with 1) the globalization of economic activity [...] and 2) the increasingly marked racialization of labour-market fragmentation'. As a result, for example, she notes, 'components of the production process in the advanced global information economy that take place in immigrant work environments are components not recognized as part of the global information economy' (Sassen, 1998, p.87).

Sassen's general point is that there is a systematic, structural relation between globalization and the feminization of wage labour, and that both 'immigration and offshore production are ways of securing a low-wage labour force and of fighting the demands of organized workers in developed countries' (Sassen, 1998, p.111). We would be wrong to think that modernized industrial processes in a sophisticated globalized economy have spelled the end of sweatshop-type exploitation, even though multinational-owned component manufactures often have a better record on employment conditions and wages than do domestic sweatshops. Sassen contends that, on the contrary, the 'growth of labour-intensive manufacturing plants in several Third World countries, as well as the growing use of sweatshops and industrial homework via subcontracting both in the Third World and in highly industrialized countries, all point to the' continuing use of these forms in modern contexts (Sassen, 1998, p.115). Steans confirms that calling home-working the 'informal sector' of the economy misrepresents the numbers of women involved in it. It is not outside or parallel to the formal sector, but is an integral part of the global market economy.

Steans refers to a further aspect of global political economy, previously unrecognized, when globalization is defined very narrowly. This is 'the rapid growth of sex tourism, or prostitution, which is linked to the expansion of the tourist industry' as well as with the location of major centres for multinational corporations and regional centres for global organizations. She observes that in countries such as 'Thailand, the Philippines, the Caribbean, West Africa and Brazil, the growing sex industry', largely but not only involving women, 'is linked closely with the expansion of tourism and is inextricably linked to the problems of debt and development strategies'. Indeed, she notes, 'prostitution is itself becoming a globally traded commodity' (Steans, 2000, p.368).

Steans also notes that the 'gender-specific impact of global restructuring, structural adjustment, debt and the feminization of poverty have long been recognized' by feminists. Further analysis of 'gender relations is needed because ideas about the "naturalness" of forms of gender inequality are integral to understanding how the global economy functions' (Steans, 1998, p.134). For instance, she notes that in the paid sector, while 'women now make up some 41 per cent of paid workers in developed countries and 34 per cent worldwide', it is 'still the case that on average they earn 30–40 per cent less than men for comparable work'. In addition, women as a group tend to work longer hours than men, as well as accounting for more poorly-paid part-time work. In the unpaid and informal sectors, women account for a higher proportion of workers in these sectors, 'though much of this work is unrecorded and so invisible' (Steans, 1998, p.134). Sassen confirms the 'discrimination in pay for women and the high incidence of gender-type occupations' (Sassen, 1998, p.85), for instance in garment, shoe, and toy manufacture, electronics assembly and food processing.

Another version of the argument about those who lose most begins from the positive view of globalization but argues that it creates a number of losers in the process. In this view, the losers are those who by choice or lack of resources are excluded from the benefits of global trade. National economies without developed financial, communications, production and commercial structures find it difficult or impossible to participate in globalization and therefore receive much less private investment capital to help them break out from the cycle of poverty. The link between involvement in trade and receipt of foreign investment is displayed in Table 3.1 below.

TABLE 3.1   Economic globalization indicators, 1998

Economic group	Trade in goods (% of GDP)	Trade in goods (% of goods GDP)	Gross private capital flows (% of GDP)	Gross foreign direct investment (% of GDP)
Low income economies	8.3	62.5	2.0	0.9
Middle	22.1	98.9	6.4	1.6
High	38.3	95.1	22.3	5.7

Source: World Bank, 2000

The figure in the first column, for the trade in goods as a percentage of the GDP, gives a general indication of the extent to which a state's trading in goods is important to its economy. Of more significance, however, is the figure in the second column. This assesses the importance of trading in goods in terms of the overall value of goods being domestically produced. In other words, when services and other elements are excluded, these figures produce an indication of the relative importance of trade to the manufacturing sector.

ACTIVITY 3.4

What does Table 3.1 tell us about the relationship between involvement in global trade and capital investment?

COMMENT

The table shows that the higher the income of the country, the greater the significance of trade in manufactured goods and the higher the investment flows. Among the high income economies, gross private capital flows have reached 22.3 per cent (this is not shown by the table, but it is actually double the figure of ten years previous), while the low income economies remain at 2 per cent. The figures for foreign direct investment similarly show the greater significance of this to the high than to the low income economies.

SUMMARY

The globalist view on economic globalization.

- A series of interrelated drivers of change is leading to the integration of the world economy.

- These drivers are lower trade barriers, increasing financial flows, improved communications, technological advances, and increased labour mobility.

- The result is that economic processes are increasingly 'stretched', the flows and networks of economic interaction are 'intensified', economies are 'interpenetrated' and a new 'global infrastructure' is developing.

- Global trade is increasing, production of goods may involve contributions from a number of states at different production stages, foreign investment is increasing, tourism and international communications are rising rapidly.

- The process is inevitable, economic factors determine the political and cultural, and economic evidence is the most significant.

- Positive globalists see all states and peoples benefiting in the long term.

- Pessimistic globalists see threats to a range of groups, including the poor of the southern hemisphere, unskilled workers in the North, women, and all of us as victims of pollution.

4 THE TRANSFORMATIONALIST VIEW ON ECONOMIC GLOBALIZATION

● ●

I think that in many respects, globalization is still superficial [...]. It seems to me that the real layer of globalization is restricted to the capital markets. In most other areas, institutions remain intensely local. Trade, for example, is still predominantly regional [...] Most companies are predominantly national, and certainly governments remain very national.

(Fukuyama, 2001, p.1)

The question is 'whether a single borderless global economy exists today; the driving forces behind global economic integration; the extent to which states or global markets are in control of socio-economic life; and the limits to progressive economic policy and the welfare state under conditions of economic globalization.'

(Held and McGrew, 2000, p.249)

The transformationalist view is that the phenomenon of globalization can be harnessed. The transformationalist position rejects the blanket generalizations made about the inevitability of globalization by both the positive and pessimistic globalists. This case is that the strength of global economic forces needs to be recognized, but that significant scope remains for states to resist them and negotiate controls over them – to transform globalization.

According to this viewpoint, economic globalization is happening (though not necessarily in the form ascribed by the globalists) but the knock-on consequences for politics and culture are not predetermined. They interpret differently from the globalists the link between economics on the one hand and politics and culture on the other. They would argue that, whereas the globalists see economic matters *determining* what goes on in the political and cultural realms, states and cultural communities still have the agency to either embrace or resist change. According to this view, political and cultural groupings are shaped by but not fully determined by economic conditions. The relationship between economic, political and cultural affairs is more complex than the globalists allow. As Fukuyama suggests in the quote above, governments still have the capacity to have an impact on global trading patterns. In this view the consequences of global economic activity are complex and unpredictable, and their effects may be very uneven. They believe that it is possible for states to work together to exercise some controls over global economic institutions, and that there is no inevitability that multinational corporations will dominate the global economy. To understand the global economy it is necessary to identify global economic pressures, but also to study how individual and groups of states react to them.

FIGURE 3.7   States still shape economic decision making: Bush and Schroeder at the G8 summit, 2002

One example of the transformationalist view argues that 'while economic globalization may have imposed new constraints upon welfare regimes, it has at the same time generated new demands which invite, not the extinction of the welfare state, but its continuing reform'. Globalization is thus leading to an opportunity for 'redefining the role and functions of national government, emphasizing its potential strategic coordinating role – the intelligent state or the competition state – as opposed to the interventionist, redistributive state of the post-war era'. Such government programmes 'stress investment in human capital and technical skills – to make national economies more competitive – as against the provision of "passive" welfare benefits' (Held and McGrew, 2000, p.250).

While transformationalists argue that governments are the main agents that can harness globalization, they also emphasize the importance of networks facilitated by the Internet. For example, some feminists argue that globalization offers the opportunity for women and indigenous women's movements to co-ordinate campaigning groups on economic issues of common concern on a transnational basis. Sassen argues that the 'needs and agendas of women are not necessarily defined exclusively by state borders' and that 'we are seeing the formation of cross-border solidarities and notions of membership rooted in gender, sexuality, and feminism' (Sassen, 1998, p.100). Feminist movements have long recognized the need and the capacity to tackle problems such as the feminization of poverty and the negative effects of processes of global economic restructuring on women and families, as occurring in particular localities within a global context. As Steans argues, processes 'of structural adjustment, the reform of **GATT**, and privatisation have all become global gender issues and been addressed in international forums in recent years' (Steans, 1998, p.79). More broadly, Brah *et al.* argue that

> the last few years have also seen strengthened activities of citizen groups, increasing networking and collaboration among groups in the North and the South, and a cross-fertilization of ideas and interests in issues including the environment, programmes towards economic and social equality, human rights, and women's rights.
>
> (Brah *et al.*, 1999, p.13)

Transformationalists will in particular point to the successful development of regional economic groupings that enable particular states to benefit from greater economic activity without succumbing to unlimited market pressures. As Hugh Mackay points out in Chapter 2, the world can be divided into a number of regions that have their own internal dynamics as well as global ties. *Regionalization* can be seen in this view as a way in which international trade and investment are increasing, but within more limited confines than the globalists would suggest. Economic activity certainly stretches across state frontiers, but states retain some ability to negotiate with others to establish rules for trade and to place their own regulations on what can be traded.

So what kind of evidence do the transformationalists find significant? Supporters of this view identify three main regional trading blocs which are seen to dominate trade flows: (a) the North American Free Trade Agreement (NAFTA) based on the USA, (b) the European Union, and (c) East Asia based on Japan. Figures produced by the European Commission and the United Nations suggest that most trade takes place *within* rather than *between* these blocs so that only about 10 per cent of the output of each was actually exported in 1995. Moreover, outside participation in the financial systems in terms of the ownership of foreign assets was also relatively insignificant (Thompson, 2000).

The continuing relative importance of **intra-regional trade** as opposed to **inter-regional trade** is displayed in Table 3.2.

GATT

The General Agreement on Tariffs and Trade (GATT), established in 1947, conducted eight 'rounds' of multinational discussions aimed at reducing state restrictions on international trade. It was an important organization involved in international economic governance, along with the World Bank, the World Trade Organization (WTO) and the G8, etc. GATT was absorbed into the WTO in 1995.

Inter- and intra-regional trade

Inter-regional trade refers to the exchange of goods and services *between* regions, while intra-regional trade is that which takes place *within* a region.

TABLE 3.2   Merchandise trade by region (per cent)

	Exports from					Imports to				
	1963	1973	1983	1993	1999	1963	1973	1983	1993	1999
(a) Japan										
N. America	30.2	28.7	32.0	31.1	32.6	35.6	29.5	23.1	26.5	24.3
W. Europe	13.3	17.9	15.8	18.1	18.9	10.0	10.6	8.8	15.3	15.4
Asia	34.9	31.6	31.0	40.0	39.5	28.2	34.5	32.6	40.3	44.4
(b) N. America										
N. America	25.4	33.5	34.2	35.6	39.6	34.3	36.6	28.8	27.1	27.0
W. Europe	27.6	24.8	21.6	20.2	19.4	24.3	23.9	18.6	18.0	19.1
Asia	17.6	19.9	21.5	25.0	21.1	15.9	21.7	29.8	37.1	34.2
(c) W. Europe										
N. America	8.8	8.6	8.4	8.0	9.9	13.9	9.6	8.9	8.2	8.4
W. Europe	64.1	69.2	65.2	68.6	69.1	56.1	64.3	61.8	68.2	67.6
Asia	7.6	5.3	5.8	8.9	7.5	7.0	6.3	7.5	12.0	12.2

Source: adapted from WTO, 2002, tables II.3, II.4, II.5

ACTIVITY 3.5

What general patterns does Table 3.2 reveal about intra-regional trade?

COMMENT

The table does reveal some volatility in intra- and inter-regional trade patterns, but:

1 Intra-regional trade is particularly important for Western Europe with approximately two-thirds of its merchandise imports and exports being intra-regional throughout the period. (See the penultimate row where the percentage of trade within W. Europe is between 56.1 per cent and 69.2 per cent for both imports and exports throughout the period.)

2 Japan has increased the importance of its trading relationship with the rest of Asia, while North America remains of growing significance to it in terms of exports.

3 North America has steadily increased its intra-regional significance in terms of exports, but is increasing its share of imports from outside the region.

4 In general the significance of intra-regional merchandise trade is growing, and that would be used as evidence by 'transformationalists' to support their position.

According to transformationalists, there are many examples where countries have undoubtedly participated in and benefited from global economic integration but have nevertheless been able to take steps to limit certain aspects of economic globalization. In September 1998 the Malaysian government reacted to the Asian financial crisis by imposing emergency controls on the movement of capital. France has imposed limits on the import of American cultural products; for example, there is a quota on the import of US films, preventing some American cable channels from being carried by French cable providers. Despite considerable WTO pressure for free trade in agriculture, France has also managed to retain considerable subsidies for its farmers through the European Union's Common Agricultural Policy (CAP). Even the USA, which is generally seen as a major promoter of globalization, has placed restrictions on trade when the interests of its own industries have been threatened by cheap imports from abroad. In 2002, for example, the USA threatened a trade war with Europe by placing restrictions on steel imports that it saw as endangering the American steel industry.

Inter-state co-operation to resist unwanted global developments has also been evident. In the wake of Asian, South American and Russian financial crises in the 1990s, various countries collaborated to develop a 'new financial architecture' which would help prevent or limit the effects of similar financial crises in the future. This included the stronger regulation of banking sectors and the greater sharing of information about national economic circumstances.

SUMMARY

The transformationalist view on economic globalization.

- Significant changes to the international economy are taking place, but the globalization process is not inevitable.

- Economic factors shape or influence the political and the cultural, but they do not determine them.

- Governments still have the capacity to have an impact on global trading patterns.

- States work together to exercise control over global economic institutions and multinational corporations.

- To understand the global economy it is necessary to study both economic pressures and the way states react to them.

- The strength of regional economic groupings shows how states can benefit from economic activity without submitting to unfettered global pressures.

- States can and do co-operate to establish mutually beneficial rules for trade.

- There are many examples which show states taking action to limit potentially adverse effects of economic globalization.

- Some feminists have seen opportunities for the advancement of women's rights in co-operation across frontiers.

5 THE INTER-NATIONALIST CRITIQUE OF ECONOMIC GLOBALIZATION

● ●

Some observers fear that the September 11 attacks, like the assassination that triggered World War I and ended the last globalization surge, will usher in an era of barbed-wire borders and populism. Last year, the World Bank finds, trade underwent 'one of the most severe decelerations in modern times'.

(Kurlantzick and Allen, 2002, p.1)

Long-distance commerce has existed for centuries and in some cases even millennia. Ancient Babylon and the Roman Empire knew forms of long-distance lending and trade, for example. Shipments between Arabia and China via South and South-East Asia transpired with fair regularity more than a thousand years ago [...] Banks based in Italian city-states maintained (temporary) offices along long-distance trade routes as early as the twelfth century.

(Scholte, 2001, pp.520–2)

According to inter-nationalists, the concept of economic globalization 'has been oversold and its impact overstated' (DeLong, 1999, p.6), and that the significance of globalization as a radically new phase has been exaggerated. This marks a rejection of the belief, shared by the globalist and transformationalist positions, that economic globalization is now a fact of life. The inter-nationalist view emphasizes the *continuities* with international economic patterns in the past. It argues that international economic interactions are nothing new and that there is certainly no inevitable evolutionary path towards a single global economy. This perspective recognizes that changes have been taking place in the extent of international economic interdependency and integration between economic agents, but considers that these have been monitored by state-based economies and regional groupings of economies to ensure their value for those involved (Thompson, 2000, p.124). Such changes have not undermined the capacity for national economic management. To the inter-nationalist position, the international economy and its governance is seeing a growing and deepening international connectedness in trade and investment, which is compatible with an open world economy of inter-linked trading nations.

According to this view, then, growing and deepening international links in trade and investment are accompanied by the continued dominance of independent state-based economic units. National economies remain a viable and indeed the primary economic category in the international world (Thompson, 2000, p.89). Like the transformationalists, inter-nationalists argue that the evidence is that trade remains predominantly regional, but unlike the transformationalists they look to developments within national *economies* rather than by *states* to explain it. Most companies and consumer markets remain largely national. In consequence, inter-nationalists highlight that the pattern of rich and poor countries and their regional dependencies broadly continues as before, with any changes in positioning due less to *global* economic forces than to *local* or *regional* economies.

5.1 Economic globalization as a continuing debate

Inter-nationalists offer serious arguments about both the adequacy of theory and the validity of empirical evidence. The strongest argument about theory is that the debate about globalization remains and will continue to be just that, a debate. Globalization is not a self-evident reality, but a debate about how to assess the significance of different phenomena and processes. But because many speak and act as though it is a fact, globalization is in danger of being taken for granted as true. Inter-nationalists argue, however, that globalization is not an inexorable, unified and irreversible process, but is *constructed* by globalists and transformationalists as an explanation of certain selected economic effects, and to serve particular interests. These economic effects remain open to other, less over-dramatic understandings. While representing itself as a neutral description of the world as it is, globalization is 'an image in which the world is being made' (Brah *et al.*, 1999, p.8). According to inter-nationalists, the globalists and transformationalists jump the gun by addressing the question, 'how can we understand globalization?', when they haven't yet conclusively demonstrated a positive answer to the prior question, 'do these changes add up to globalization or not?' Inter-nationalists answer 'no' to this prior question.

Brah *et al.*, drawing on the work of the renowned geographer Doreen Massey, argue that one of the most influential uses of the term globalization (directly relevant to the discussion of economic globalization) has been to reinterpret the West's story about itself. They argue that the Eurocentric 'classic story of modernity' now passes itself off as globally 'universal', so that colonial and post-colonial histories have been absorbed and appropriated into the dominant story of the West as a narrative of European progress. The history of European economic and technological 'progress' becomes the pre-given backdrop. Moreover, the image of globalization as unfettered movement can 'easily be conflated with the idea of "free trade", a conflation which then becomes a powerful alibi for countries of the North to impose – via institutions such as the IMF, the World Bank, and the World Trade Organization – programmes of structural adjustment on countries of the South, with hardship for the poor, the excluded and especially for women'. In this way, they say, 'the powerful countries of the North are able to exercise their power by pleading powerlessness in the face of the supposed globalizing market forces' (Brah *et al.*, 1999, p.8). Some globalists and transformationalists continue to think uncritically about international economic activity on this basis, ignoring rather than seeking to accommodate other possible stories.

A series of feminist arguments challenges how the economy and the international sphere has been constructed – what has been counted in and what has been left out. Sassen argues that 'the mainstream account of economic globalization is confined to a very narrow analytic terrain', one which 'excludes a whole range of workers, firms, and sectors that do not fit the prevalent images of globalization' (Sassen, 1998, p.82).

Similarly Steans notes that by 'concentrating on the impersonal structures of states and markets, it is not possible to see how women's activities have been demoted to the "private" sphere' (Steans, 1998, pp.132–3). She remarks that gender 'is rendered invisible because of the way in which both "economic" and "political" activity has conventionally been defined. In capitalist economies the market is viewed as the core of economic activity'. In consequence, participation 'in the labour force and the inclusion of production in measurements of global economic activity has been defined only in relation to the market, or to the performance of work for pay or profit'. It follows that 'unremunerated work and the person performing it (usually a woman) is not included because it is not part of the market of paid exchanges for goods and services and so not viewed as economically significant' (Steans, 1998, p.133). Sassen underlines the point that economic globalization activities can be specified as male-gendered insofar as they have 'the cultural properties and power dynamics that we have historically associated with men of power' (Sassen, 1998, p.82).

Steans highlights another dimension of the point that the economic realm has been defined too narrowly when she outlines the feminist critique of the boundary economists have drawn between the public and private spheres. Current feminist analyses in international political economy, she notes, are engaged in working towards new understandings of 'economic' and 'political' which will highlight the links between what has conventionally been seen as separate. Feminist research is now concerned with recovering the role of women in international economic activity, which cover a range of kinds of unpaid work in the 'private' sphere of family and the domestic economy.

Some environmentalists argue that the term globalization gets in the way of attempts to control the effects of economic activity in pollution and global warming, and keeps sustainability off the agenda. While governments can hide behind the image of an inevitable process of globalization for which they are not responsible, they can avoid taking the measures which are economically costly in the short term that would help to control and regulate environmental damage.

Many political conservatives are also critical of the inevitability and desirability of globalization. They express a strong loyalty to the nation-state and wish to sustain existing political and cultural structures, seeing them as fundamental to people's identity and well-being. They also believe that governments have the power and duty to resist what they see as a challenge to traditional ways of life.

A further argument relates to the constructed nature of our dominant idea of economic globalization and the criticism of what is described as 'racialized forms of globalization'. Western-inspired, differently-valued notions of West and East, friend and enemy, self and other, security and threat, as well as North and South, and a hierarchical distinction between 'European' and 'non European', continue to inform economic decisions by governments and companies. In this way dominant meanings of globalization have not recognized sufficiently the formative influence exercised by colonialism in the development of ideas about what is distinctive about European modernity. More broadly, to understand investment, trade and migration fully, we need to look at cultural, historical and social factors. Economic decisions do not exist outside culture but are always socially embedded. An example of the significance of social and cultural values in evaluating economic activity concerns the fall of communism in Eastern Europe. After 1989, 'previously illegal activities such as trading, currency speculation, business ventures, and profit-making came to be' redefined and revalued, and are now 'seen as indicators of enterprise and initiative' (Brah *et al.*, 1999, p.22).

5.2 Economic evidence for the inter-nationalist case on economic globalization

FIGURE 3.8   Most trade is still between the advanced economies

A set of strong arguments is also offered by inter-nationalists about economic *evidence* and the interpretation to be placed on evidence. Inter-nationalists argue that globalists misrepresent historical trends when they focus only on developments since the middle of the twentieth century. Inter-nationalists point out that the general increase in the level of international trade over the past 50 years only marks a return to around the level that had been attained prior to the First World War. Evidence shows, for example, that world merchandise exports in 1913 equalled about 12 per cent of world domestic product, shrinking to about 7 per cent in 1950, rising again to 12 per cent in the 1970s and about 17 per cent in the 1990s (Grieco and Ikenberry, 2002, p.2). Similarly, US exports and imports as a percentage of American GDP exceeded 20 per cent just after the First World War, fell back to 8 per cent in the 1930s and only exceeded its previous high point in the mid 1990s. So world trade has increased as domestic output has gone up.

ACTIVITY 3.6

TABLE 3.3   Ratio of merchandise trade to GDP

	1913	1950	1973	1995	2000
France	35.4	21.2	29.0	36.6	46.9
Germany	35.1	20.1	35.2	38.7	55.8
Japan	31.4	16.9	18.3	14.1	15.2
Netherlands	103.6	70.2	80.1	83.4	106.9
UK	44.7	36.0	39.3	42.6	43.0
USA	11.2	7.0	10.5	19.0	20.7

2000 figures calculated from OECD, *National Accounts*, 2002, country tables.
Source: Thompson, 2000, p.97

Look at the figures in Table 3.3. What do they tell us about the differences between countries, and the long-term trends?

COMMENT _____

The differences between countries have, roughly, been maintained. The long-term trends have remained roughly stable, with similar levels in 1913 as in 2000. This reinforces the inter-nationalist contention that the degree of trade openness was about the same in 1913 as it was in 2000, and goes against the globalist view that the intensification of flows leads to the greater interpenetration of economies.

While globalists regard global economic forces as a fundamental dimension driving political and cultural forms, and transformationalists identify a continuing role for state governments, inter-nationalists see national economies as still the key to understanding what is happening. In this view world trade and investment have developed *because of* not *despite* self-interested decisions by national economies. Hirst and Thompson develop a powerful case against the new global economy thesis on the basis of their 'careful analytical distinction between the idea of an international economy (links between separate national economies) and a universal global economy (economic organization without borders)' (Held and McGrew, 2000, p.250).

The idea of an international economy is based on the notion of *interdependence*, whereby activities in one place have effects in other places. The idea of a global economy, by contrast, is based on the stronger connection of *integration*, such that effects in two places are due to the same event. State-based economies have co-ordinated the advantages of more prosperous life-styles, increasing specialization, importing valuable technology, and attracting external investment to create jobs, and have therefore been supportive of growing international connections. However, when any of these developments begins to threaten the interests of a national economy, action is taken to prevent or limit their effects. In 2002, for example, the US government unilaterally imposed an 8–30 per cent levy on imported steel in order to protect its own ailing steel industry, with President Bush claiming that US producers needed time to adjust and 'compete on a level playing field' (*The Guardian*, 6 March 2002). The significance of this levy lies in the fact that the United States is often seen as the prime mover of, and as deriving the most benefit from, the globalization process. Thus this action by the USA can be seen as evidence of the continued importance of the self-interest of states and does not support the view for the irresistible pressures of faceless and uncontrolled global economic forces.

Another example of the inter-nationalists' interpretation of how international economic governance works is offered by recent disputes over agriculture, with three groups of countries arguing within the WTO for global policies that favour their own agricultural interests: the European Union, the USA, and the Cairns Group (led by Australia, New Zealand, and Canada). The Cairns Group, whose agricultural production tends to be large scale, has argued for total free trade in agricultural produce, with no trade barriers and no forms of subsidy. The EU has taken an opposed position, reflecting the much smaller scale of its productive units, and supports aid being given to farmers working in difficult environments. The USA position falls between the other two, seeing free agricultural trade as beneficial to its Midwest farmers, but also seeing dangers from open competition with other large-scale producers. When the WTO was established, there was agreement to cut subsidies and trade tariffs on agriculture, but the EU was able to negotiate concessions which meant that the full effect of such measures would be delayed for a number of years. This allowed plans for rural diversification to be implemented to cushion the blow to their farmers. Inter-nationalists would argue on the basis of this evidence that the net result is that moves towards liberalization of international trade are only accepted by wealthy national economies if they correspond to their 'national interest'.

As well as the important distinction between an international and a global economy, inter-nationalists make another important point in arguing that the term '*multinational corporation*' (a key term in the globalist argument) needs to be critically examined and not confused with the idea of a '*transnational corporation*' (Hirst and Thompson, 1999). While MNCs spread production across different countries, inter-nationalists point out that many such companies maintain a clear national base from which their operations are co-ordinated. The internationalization of the modern business firm began as early as the 1850s (Thompson, 2000, p.104). Such organizations clearly attempt to extend their activities beyond their national base, but they remain closely identified with a particular national economy whose authorities could effectively monitor or regulate their activities.

Thus, according to the inter-nationalist case, there are far fewer genuinely *multi*-national corporations than has been supposed. These few may be more accurately described as '*transnational corporations*' (TNCs) which are 'disembodied' from any national base, and which have a more genuinely international organization and personnel (Thompson, 2000, p.103). While both MNCs and TNCs produce and market internationally and seek to maximize profits by locating production wherever it can most cheaply and efficiently be undertaken, TNCs have full foreign manufacturing capacity without a national base, whereas MNCs manufacture only parts of their end product at overseas locations. Inter-nationalists hold that this distinction, between multinational corporations that are still state-based and a much smaller number of genuinely transnational corporations, fits the evidence better than the interpretation put forward by the globalists as to the way the international economy is developing. Inter-nationalists have argued that in practice examples of TNCs are few. Grahame Thompson has suggested that Rupert Murdoch's News Corporation Ltd and the Swiss–Swedish electrical equipment manufacturer Asea Brown Boveri (ABB) can fit this picture, but few others do (Thompson, 2000, p.103). Honda, which is often cited as a key example of the contemporary internationalized firm does have many subsidiaries in European countries and has a complex production process that is integrated across countries and continents. Components are moved between factories in this production chain. However, two-thirds of Honda's assets and sales in 1998 were still located in Japan, and so it is still a Japanese corporation with a clear home base from which it can be regulated (Thompson, 2000, p.106).

Following on from this distinction between multinational and transnational corporations, inter-nationalists develop the view that, while the growth in trade has led to international *interdependency*, the increase in capital flows has not been sufficient to warrant the assessment of economic *integration*. International trade and overseas investment are the two key building blocks for a genuinely international economy. Only with proper economic integration would it be fair to claim that globalization has occurred. The upshot is that no amount of deepening and intensification of *trade* relations between economies will lead, on its own, to economic globalization. No matter how 'open' economies are to the impacts of international trade, the scale and density of international trade is only one of the two indicators of globalization. A properly globalized system can only occur if economic integration is produced via massive increases in overseas investment (capital flows) by TNCs. Moreover, it is the capital flows between the richest **G8** countries that have the biggest impact. In the investment relationships between these advanced economies FDI does not figure strongly. Inter-nationalists go on to demonstrate that while international trade has increased massively, overseas investment flows through proper TNCs using FDI remains marginal, and capital flows as a whole have moved up and down but are no higher at the present time than they were a century ago. Inter-nationalists argue that globalists, by taking increases in FDI as the most significant indicator of international economic integration (and so of globalization), fail to take into account the more important measure of **capital flows** as a whole. This is the heart of inter-nationalist arguments concerning economic evidence. They are 'inter-nationalist' because they argue that capital flows between the advanced states remains the most important indicator of what is happening in the international economic system.

The inter-nationalist critique of the globalist perspective in particular thus makes two essential claims. It rebuts the view that economic globalization has crucially involved a sharp increase in genuine TNCs and **foot-loose capital** (Thompson, 2000, p.109). And it argues that international economic governance remains in the hand of groups of national economies such as the G8. The advanced economies remain in control of decisions about the direction in which economic matters should develop. Inter-nationalists share the concerns of many pessimistic globalists that current developments favour the strong and threaten the vulnerable. National economies and regional groups of economies with high incomes (expressed in GDP) such as those centred on the USA, Japan and the EU have the political power to block or at least postpone and dilute moves in global trade that threaten their interests. These bodies are able to shape the direction and pace of globalization and decide whether or not developing new institutions and rules should go ahead. Meanwhile the weak, poor and isolated economies with low GDP are as vulnerable economically to the rules of the powerful as they were politically to imperial powers in the past. They are given the stark choice of accepting membership of a global system, which effectively rules out their ability to protect their own industries and markets, or to opt out of the system and remain in limbo with little investment or trade opportunities. In practice, inter-nationalists would argue, this has meant increased trade for many national economies without many of the anticipated benefits.

G8

The group of eight main industrialized economies. These are: the USA, Japan, Germany, the UK, France, Italy, Canada and the Russian Federation. Developed from the G5 (USA, Germany, Japan, UK and France) and the G7 (USA, Germany, Japan, UK, France, Italy and Canada). Annual meetings of the government leaders of these countries, and more frequent meetings between their finance ministers, are designed to increase economic collaboration between them on international economic problems.

Capital flows

The amount of capital (borrowing and lending) that moves from one country to another in a set time period such as a year. Capital flows can be either physical or speculative (as in the case of the 'rogue trader' Nick Leeson). These capital flows are sometimes expressed as international investment.

Foot-loose capital

Productive potential that is not tied to a particular location by virtue of an economic need to be close to sources of raw material, specialized labour, or market.

ACTIVITY 3.7

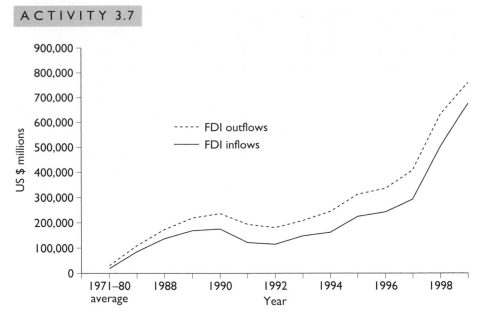

FIGURE 3.9   FDI inflows and outflows for OECD countries, 1971–99
Source: OECD, 2000

OECD
This stands for the Organisation for Economic Co-operation and Development which consists of 30 member states who share a commitment to democratic government and the market economy. It is best known for its publications and statistics on a range of economic and social issues.

Figure 3.9 shows FDI inflows and outflows for all the OECD countries. This refers to the combined outflows to and inflows from each of the OECD countries, regardless of where the FDI was going to or coming from (including other OECD countries). What does the graph tell us about FDI flows over time?

COMMENT

The graph illustrates clearly the dip in the total FDI as a result of the global recession in the early 1990s. It then clearly shows the very significant increase in FDI in the late 1990s. Much of this was through mergers and acquisitions. It can be anticipated that OECD figures will show a significant fall in FDI in the first years of the twenty-first century as the world economy faltered.

Even if it can clearly be established that FDI is on the increase, we need then to establish its direction. The globalists' case would be challenged if it could be established that the direction of FDI were overwhelmingly between similar developed OECD states and having little effect on other parts of the world.

Hirst and Thompson argue persuasively that, on the basis of these key economic criteria, what we are facing is much more a 'conjunctural change toward greater international trade and investment within an existing set of economic relations' as opposed to 'the development of a new economic structure' (Hirst and Thompson, 1999, p.7).

Figures from the United Nations Conference on Trade and Development (UNCTAD) offer support for this perspective. In 1999 for almost all developing countries imports expanded faster than exports, resulting in a deterioration of their trade balance. While the share of developed countries in world income increased from less than 73 per cent in 1980 to 77 per cent in 1999, that of developing countries stagnated at around 20 per cent (UNCTAD, 2002, Chapter 3). The key to this situation lies in the particular goods that are being exported. The UNCTAD report suggests that the developed countries are exporting what it calls 'dynamic' products with high global demand and productivity potential, while developing countries remain locked into the export of goods with sluggish global demand and persistent potential for excess supply. Table 3.4 shows the share of the world market held by developing countries and the main exporters of what UNCTAD identified as the ten most market-dynamic products for 1998.

TABLE 3.4 Exports of market-dynamic products

Product group	Share of world market held by developing countries (%)	Main exporting countries (% share)
Transistors and semiconductors	46	USA (17), Japan (15)
Computers	36	USA (13), Singapore (13)
Parts of computers, office machines	38	USA (17), Japan (14)
Optical instruments	30	Japan (22), USA (17)
Perfumery and cosmetics	10	France (28), USA (12)
Silk	87	China (70), Germany (9)
Knitted undergarments	57	China (16), USA (8)
Plastic articles	23	USA (14), Germany (13)
Electric power machinery	37	USA (11), Germany (10)
Musical instruments and records	18	USA (20), Japan (12)

Source: adapted from UNCTAD, 2002, Table 3.2

ACTIVITY 3.8

Consider what Table 3.4 tells us about the relationship between developed and developing countries in terms of exports.

COMMENT

The table shows that developing countries are enjoying a share in the markets for some dynamic products, but developed countries continue to dominate most markets in these goods, and significant success is limited to a few developing countries such as China. There are no examples here of African or South American countries being able to derive much advantage. Furthermore, the table hides the fact that much of the contribution of developing countries is in low-skill, low **value-added** assembly stages of global production networks, as in electronics.

Value-added
This is the increase in value which can be measured at each stage of the production process.

A C T I V I T Y   3.9

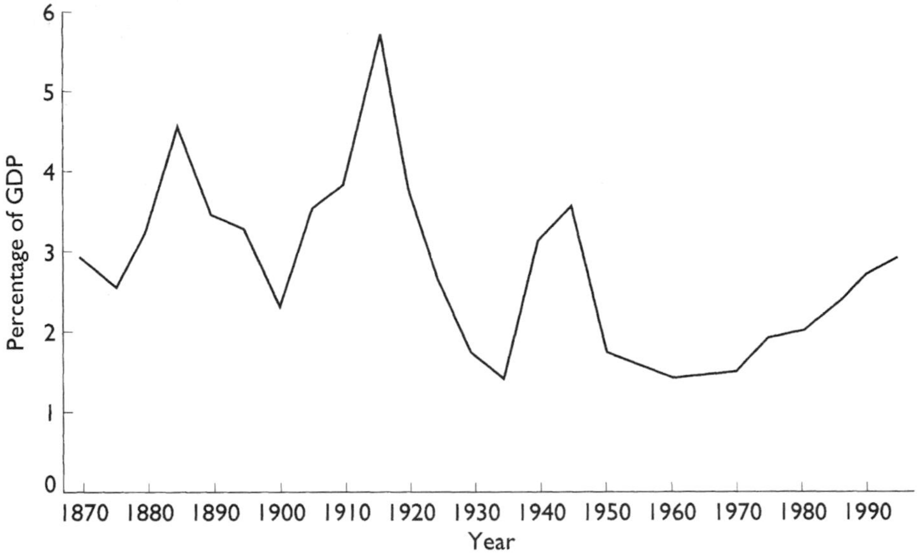

FIGURE 3.10   Total capital flows between the G7 economies, expressed as a ratio of their combined GDP, 1870–1994

Source: Institute of Development Studies, 1998

What has happened to total capital flows (as shown in Figure 3.10) between the world's richest countries?

C O M M E N T

While the investment relationship between the G7 has risen since 1960, it was greater in the earlier part of the period, and peaked in 1914. FDI contributed only around 5.2 per cent of the world's capital investment in 1995. The vast bulk of the resources to finance investment has been found from domestic sources such as savings, rather than from investment from abroad by companies and corporations. This conclusion supports the inter-nationalist case that the international financial system is far from fully integrated (Thompson, 2000, p.109).

SUMMARY

The inter-nationalist view on economic globalization.

- Whether or not globalization is happening is still a debate but there is strong evidence that its significance has been exaggerated.

- Ideas of the economy and international economy have been defined very narrowly by globalists, often ignoring the economic contribution of women.

- The continuities in the key international economic indicators (trade and investment) are much more significant than the changes.

- The phenomena labelled globalization by the globalists are really no more than the reinforcing of long-term and deeply-entrenched patterns of inequality between rich and poor regions.

- International economic governance is still directed by the stronger and richer economies and is largely in their interests.

- International bodies, such as the WTO, have powers delegated to them by national economies when it is deemed in their interests to do so.

- Trade is primarily regional, while companies and consumer markets remain predominantly national.

- The relative importance of global trade is only at the same level as it was a century ago.

- Most multinational corporations are essentially nationally based, while genuinely transnational corporations are few in number.

- Even where poorer national economies seem to be benefiting from increased production and export of goods, much of the value added at each stage of production may still accrue to the richer countries.

- Rich national economies have the capacity to adapt to meet new economic challenges.

6 CONCLUSION

The idea that we live in a world adequately described by the term globalization is a dominant one. It has been embraced by many academics, journalists, commentators and politicians. It seems to be the driving force behind the way the international economy is organized and thought about, through an emphasis on the ubiquity of free market forces and international competition. It also seems to direct what policy responses can (or more likely, cannot) be devised to respond to it. Different arguments, multiple forms of evidence, and varying interpretations of evidence, have been presented in the globalist, transformationalist and inter-nationalist cases. The argument highlighted in this chapter is the inter-nationalist one that we should remain sceptical of this trend (Thompson, 2000, p.123).

There is plenty of evidence that what is meant by the 'economy' and the 'international economy' have been defined very narrowly. The dominant way these terms are constructed favours the globalist case. Opening up the meanings of these terms to take into account the implicit but unsustainable public/private distinction that is made, the narrowness of the definition of 'rational economic man', the extent of the inequalities faced by women and others, and the real nature of migration and offshore production, would broaden out the debate about globalization and reinforce the inter-nationalist case.

In terms of the key structural indicators in the inter-nationalist case's use of the economic evidence there does not seem to have been such a dramatic move towards a fully global economy as is often assumed (Thompson, 2000, p.123). The analysis of both trade interdependency and investment integration discloses that whilst there has undoubtedly been some increase in these over the past 50 years, the levels of capital flows in particular does not give us reason to conclude that globalization is upon us. Moreover, the activity of most international corporations is still best summed up as that of MNCs rather than TNCs. Indeed, in many ways the international economy is not as globalized as it was before the First World War.

To embrace a strong economic globalization thesis leads policy makers to disempower themselves and to settle for a reduced set of expectations of what can still be done to manage the international economy and, perhaps equally importantly, to manage any single national economy so as to protect the living standards of its citizens. Indeed, at its most extreme, the globalist position, remembering the globalization continuum set out in Figure 3.1, implies that the category of a national economy is no longer a relevant one (Thompson, 2000, p.123). The inter-nationalist critique argues that this is not the case. For those not completely persuaded by the idea of a totally free market system as proposed by the positive globalists, the message in this chapter is 'beware of the strong globalization thesis!' (Thompson, 2000, p.123).

As Thompson notes, the inter-nationalist argument 'focuses on the role of national economies as key *agents* in the international economic system, where the international economic system is the *structure* in which those agents exist. This structure is made up of the international market system' that is thought by globalists to dictate to the agents what they can and cannot do. The implication of the inter-nationalist argument put forward here is that 'there is still much more room for manoeuvre for these agents in the international system than is often recognized' (Thompson, 2000, pp.123–4). In addition, international companies can also be designated as agents in the system, most of which are still embedded in national territorial bases. As a result, the inter-nationalist approach argues, agents such as national economies and their governments, particularly of wealthy states, can (if they choose) 'monitor, manage and control these companies to a greater extent than is recognized' by the globalist (and even transformationalist) position (Thompson, 2000, p.124). Another central plank of the inter-nationalist position is that the degree of *interdependence* in the *international* economy does not amount to the *integration* of a *global* economy. From this it follows that the relevance of national economies as the main powers responsible for international economic governance and decision making remains. These agents are 'not as totally beholden to the anonymous forces of the market as they might be' (Thompson, 2000, p.124). In all these ways, for the inter-nationalist approach, structure does not dominate agency to the extent that it does for the globalist position.

REFERENCES

Albert, M. (2001) *What Are We For?*, Znet, 6 September, at http://www.globalpolicy.org/globaliz/econ/2001/0906gbz.htm (accessed February 2002).

American Foreign Policy Association (2002) *Globalization's Last Hurrah?*, at http:www.globalpolicy.org.globaliz/define/0101.htm (accessed February 2002).

Arnold, G. (2001) 'Neo-colonialism is alive and flourishing', *West Africa*, 18–24 February 2002.

Brah, A., Hickman, M. and Mac an Ghaill, M. (1999) 'Introduction: whither "the Global?"' in Brah, A., Hickman, M. and Mac an Ghaill, M. (eds) *Global Futures. Migration, Environment and Globalization*, London, Palgrave.

DeLong, J.B. (1999) *Globalization and Neoliberalism*, at http://econ161.berkeley.edu/Econ_Articles/Reviews/alexkafka.html (accessed February 2002).

European Commission (1997) *Annual Economic Report for 1997, European Economy No.63*, Official Publication of the European Communities, Luxembourg.

Friedman, T.L. (1999) *The Lexus and the Olive Tree*, New York, Farrar, Straus and Giroux.

Fukuyama, F. (2001) 'Economic globalization and culture: a discussion with Dr Francis Fukuyama', at http://www.ml.com/wonl/forum/global.htm (accessed May 2003).

Galbraith, J.K. (1999) *The Crisis of Globalization*, at http://www.igc.apc.org/dissent/current/summer99/galbrait.html (accessed February 2002).

Grieco, J.M. and Ikenberry, G.J. (2002) 'Economic globalization and its discontents' in *State Power and World Markets*, New York, Norton, at http://www.duke.edu/-grieco/chapter6.htm (accessed February 2002).

Held, D. and McGrew, A. (eds) (2000) *Polity Global Transformations Reader*, Cambridge, Polity.

Hirst, P.Q. and Thompson, G.F. (1999) *Globalization in Question: The International Economy and the Possibilities of Governance* (2nd edn), Cambridge, Polity.

Institute of Development Studies (1998) 'Asia's Victorian financial crisis', paper presented at the Conference on the East Asian Economic Crisis, University of Sussex, Brighton, 13–14 July.

International Chamber of Commerce (2000) 'ICC brief on globalization', 22 November, at http://globalization.about.com/g:/dynamic/offsite.htm (accessed May 2003).

Kurlantzick, J. and Allen, J.T. (2002) *The Trouble With Globalism*, US News and World Report, 11 February.

Mander, J. and Barker, D. (2002) *Does Globalization Help the Poor?*, at http://www.globalpolicy.org/globaliz/econ/2002/0701.htm (accessed February 2002).

OECD (2000) *International Direct Investment Statistics Yearbook*, Paris, Organization for Economic Co-operation and Development.

OECD, *National Accounts*, Paris, Organization for Economic Co-operation and Development (quarterly).

Rally Comrades! (1997) 'Economic globalization: capitalism in the age of electronics', vol.15, no.2, at http://www.Irna.org/league/Rally/15.02/rc.15.02.global.html (accessed March 2002).

Sassen, S. (1998) *Globalization and its Discontents*, New York, New Press.

Scholte, J.A. (2001) 'Global trade and finance' in Baylis, J. and Smith, S. (eds) *The Globalization of World Politics*, Oxford, Oxford University Press.

Steans, J. (1998) *Gender and International Relations. An Introduction*, Cambridge, Polity.

Steans, J. (2000) 'The gender dimension' in Held, D. and McGrew, A. (eds).

The Economist (2001) 'Some win, some lose', 5 December.

The Quadral Group of worldwide business advisors (1996) *What is Globalization?*, at http:www.quadralgroup.com/globis.htm (accessed February 2002).

The Times of India (2002) 'Globalization hits the poor most', 14 February, at http://www.globalpolicy.org/globaliz/econ/2002/0214india.htm (accessed February 2002).

Thompson, G. (2000) 'Economic globalization?' in Held, D. (ed.) *A Globalizing World? Culture, Economics, Politics* (1st edn), London, Routledge/ The Open University.

UNCTAD (2002) *Trade and Development Report*, Geneva, United Nations Conference on Trade and Development.

Weller, C.E., Scott, R.E. and Hersh, A.S. (2002) *The Unremarkable Record of Liberalized Trade*, Briefing Paper, October, Washington, DC, Economic Policy Institute.

World Bank (2000) *World Development Indicators, 1998*, Washington, DC, World Bank.

World Bank (2001) *Globalization, Growth and Poverty: Facts, Fears and an Agenda for Action*, Draft Policy Research Report, Washington, DC, World Bank.

WTO (2000, 2002) *International Trade Statistics*, Geneva, World Trade Organization.

FURTHER READING

The three competing positions on economic globalization are represented by Reinicke (1998), which accepts the globalist thesis but argues for the establishment of new global governance mechanisms; Held *et al.* (1999), which emphasizes the transformationalist viewpoint; and by Hirst and Thompson (1999), which argues from a strong inter-nationalist position.

Held, D., McGrew, A., Goldblatt, D. and Perraton, J. (1999) *Global Transformations: Politics, Economics and Culture*, Cambridge, Polity.

Hirst, P.Q. and Thompson, G.F. (1999) *Globalization in Question: The International Economy and the Possibilities of Governance* (2nd edn), Cambridge, Polity.

Reinicke, W.H. (1998) *Global Public Policy: Governing Without Government?*, Washington, Brookings Institution Press.

Power shift: from national government to global governance?

Anthony McGrew

1 INTRODUCTION

· ·

'He was just the normal Allan', says his grandmother, Margaret. 'He got changed that night – he put on a different trackie suit. He changed out of his blue one and into a white one'

(Gillan, *The Guardian*, 6 February 1999)

Early the following morning Allan Harper – a street-wise, 13 year old Glasgow schoolboy – had been pronounced dead. Found in his favourite white 'trackie suit', in a flat on Startpoint Street, among the estates of the city's Cranhill area, Allan had achieved an unfortunate notoriety as the youngest person to die of a heroin overdose in the United Kingdom. For Jacqueline, Allan's grieving mother, Tony Blair's announcement, at the 1998 **G8** Birmingham Summit, of the most concerted global campaign ever mounted to combat the growing world trade in illicit narcotics, appeared mere rhetoric. On the outposts of the global heroin trade, in places such as Cranhill, it had been business as usual.

G8
This is the G7 group (USA, Japan, Germany, France, UK, Italy and Canada) with the addition of Russia.

FIGURE 4.1   Balcony of the flat where Allan Harper died, Cranhill, Glasgow

Several years on, even with the support of a United Nations commitment to stem the drugs trade, the G8 initiative appears to have given way to a reluctant realization that the combined efforts of the world's most powerful governments – the G8 states – may be unable to stem the growth of the illegal drugs trade. Such is the sophisticated transnational organization of this trade, estimated to exceed global flows of investment by all the world's multinational corporations combined (see Figure 4.2), that individual governments, including powerful ones like the US, appear unable to combat one of the most serious social problems to afflict both affluent and poor societies alike.

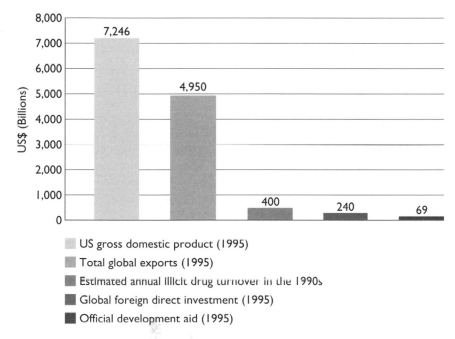

FIGURE 4.2   World international drug trade (comparative international aggregates)
Source: UNDCP, 1997

As globalization has intensified, the power of national governments to tackle it appears to have declined and international bodies lack the authority to enforce agreed policies. In effect, globalization invites the real possibility of a more unruly world as transnational forces, like the illegal drugs trade, escape the control of nation-states.

Paradoxically, it has been the G8 governments' abandonment of many national controls, in the determined pursuit of open global markets for goods, services and capital, that has created new opportunities for an illegal drugs trade to prosper. The infrastructures and systems – communication, transportation, financial, trade – that enable white Nike 'trackies' from the sweatshops of the Philippines to be sold at a handsome profit on the street markets of Glasgow also make an organized illegal drugs trade possible. Globalization is not simply an economic phenomenon – measured by the dramatic expansion of world trade or flows of 'hot money' between the major financial markets – but has equally significant social, political and human dimensions. It has enormous consequences for human security, as the life-chances and well-being of individuals and communities in distant regions of the globe become intimately connected through highly organized transnational networks over which they, or even their governments, may have little direct control. Globalization has a human face even though it is often obscured from public view.

Contemporary patterns of globalization raise the most profound questions about how modern societies are governed and – normatively speaking – how they should be governed. *Globalists* argue that in a globalized world, national governments are increasingly powerless and irrelevant. While they are too small to deal with the global problems that affect their citizens – such as global warming or the illegal drugs trade – they are too big to deal with local matters such as refuse recycling. In short, in the UK, the power of Whitehall is being eclipsed by bodies above it (the EU), below it (the Scottish Assembly) and alongside it (multinational corporations). By contrast, *inter-nationalists* maintain that the capacity of national governments to regulate the lives of their citizens and to manage global affairs has never been so extensive. Rather than the end of the nation-state, inter-nationalists conclude that globalization is reaffirming the centrality of national governments to the management of human affairs.

Transformationalists take issue with both accounts arguing that, in the global neighbourhood created by the forces of globalization, national governments are having to adapt their roles and functions. As a result, a significant reconfiguration in the power, jurisdiction, authority and legitimacy of states is underway. National governments are not so much losing power but having to adjust to a new context in which their power and sovereignty is shared and bartered among many other public and private agencies – above, below and alongside the nation-state. In the UK, this 'powershift' is expressed in the continuing controversy about national sovereignty in the context of the EU and devolved government. For transformationalists, how we are governed, by whom, in whose interests and to what ends – the classic questions of politics – have been posed afresh by the process of globalization.

In reflecting upon these matters, this chapter will extend the analysis of globalization to the specifically political realm, that is, to issues of power, authority, legitimacy and governance (the process of governing). In doing so, it will address four key questions which arise from the contemporary debate about globalization.

1   Is politics becoming globalized? To what extent have recent decades witnessed the emergence of new forms of transnational political activity and organization?

2   What are we to understand by the idea of global governance? How is it conducted, by whom and in whose interests?

3 To what extent does globalization prefigure a historic power shift from national governments and electorates to evolving systems of regional and global governance?

4 Is globalization associated with a more unruly or a more benign world order?

Note

Many of the intergovernmental and non-government organizations referred to in this chapter are known by their acronyms. While you will recognize a large number of these abbreviations, references are made to some less well-known organizations. To help you sort out the abbreviations used, a glossary of acronyms is provided at the end of the chapter.

2 POLITICS BEYOND BORDERS: FROM INTERNATIONAL TO GLOBAL POLITICS?

In trying to prevent the repetition of tragedies such as that which befell Allan Harper, the UK government has to confront daily the reality that, for the most part, the sources of the illegal drugs trade – although not the demand for the trade – lie well beyond its legal and political jurisdiction. Constructing effective policies to deal with inner-city drugs problems, and their related social consequences, needs more than simply local or national initiatives, it requires co-ordinated international action. In an interconnected world, the distinction between domestic or local, foreign or international, begins to lose its relevance. Few aspects of UK public policy can be insulated from the direct or indirect consequences of the actions and decisions of governments, corporations, consumers, citizens' groups and local communities located in other countries. As the case of the trade in narcotics illustrates, this has serious practical consequences for the choices available to British government ministers in developing appropriate policies. Should they, for instance, spend more money on drug prevention programmes in Glasgow or upon initiatives in Laos to provide the opium farmers with financial incentives to diversify into other crops?

Beyond these practical policy considerations, the accumulation of trans-border issues raises more fundamental questions. What are the limits to national power and how effective is national government when the organization of economic and social life appears systematically to transcend territorial jurisdictions? To answer such questions, we need to review briefly the core principles that have defined the constitution of modern political life since the birth of the nation-state.

2.1 Territory, politics and world order: the Westphalian Ideal

One of the most striking features of any contemporary political map of the world is the division of geo-political space into fixed bounded territorial entities. At present, humankind is organized, for political purposes, into some 190 or more exclusive communities: that is, nation-states. To us this appears natural – it's just how the world is today and has been for some time – but to cartographers of the Middle Ages, for example, it would make little sense. In that period, the world was organized around world religions and empires that lacked clear-cut political borders. Even a century ago the world map looked very different. In the Foreign and Commonwealth Office in Whitehall, it is still possible to see, fixed to an office wall, a nineteenth century world map on which much of the globe's surface is covered in a blur of pink, representing the British Empire. As mentioned in Chapter 1, maps embody assumptions about how the world is – and should be – organized politically.

ACTIVITY 4.1

Examine the map shown below. What do you think this map presumes about the (political) organization of the world?

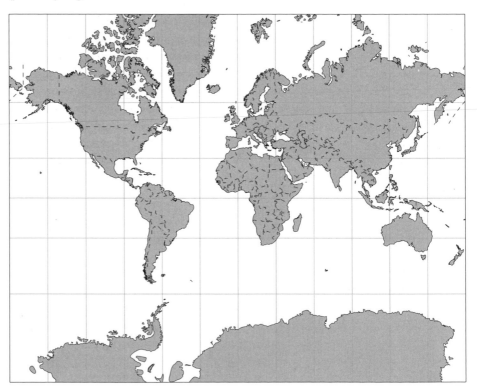

FIGURE 4.3   Political map of the world

COMMENT

My first impression is that the following five assumptions seem to inform it.

1   Humankind is organized principally into discrete territorial, political communities which are called nation-states (territoriality).

2   Within these blocks of territory, states or national governments claim supreme and exclusive authority over, and allegiance from, their peoples (sovereignty).

3   Countries appear as autonomous containers of political, social and economic activity in that fixed borders separate the domestic sphere from the world outside (autonomy).

4   States dominate the global political landscape since they control access to territory and the economic, human and natural resources therein (primacy).

5   States have to look after themselves – it's a self-help world (anarchy). One of the main functions of the state (look inside your passport) is to ensure the security and well-being of its citizens, and to protect them from outside interference.

Underlying any conventional political map of the world, according to Taylor, is a 'states as containers' conception of political life (Taylor, 1995, p.334). This has its deepest roots in the Peace of Westphalia (1648) when Europe's monarchs agreed to recognize each other's right to rule their own territories, free from outside interference. But it was only in the twentieth century, as global empires collapsed, that statehood and national self-determination finally became the sole principles by which the world's peoples came to be organized politically. Commonly referred to – because of its origins – as the 'Westphalian system', the modern system of states now colonizes the entire planet. Today, humanity is organized into separate nation-states, each jealously guarding its right to self-governance. As the continuing disputes about EU 'interference' in British domestic affairs illustrate, the question of national sovereignty remains highly charged since it is at the core of national identity.

Almost four centuries in the making, the abstract principles, norms and practices that constitute the **Westphalian system** of states have become (alongside the ideals of democracy and liberty) the central organizing features of modern political life. The Westphalian system is reproduced daily in the routine practices of states, from the conduct of international diplomacy to regular passport checks on Eurostar trains.

Westphalian system
The organization of humanity into sovereign, territorially exclusive nation-states.

In the context of global attempts to stem the illegal drugs trade, the grip of the Westphalian system on the routines of everyday politics is readily apparent. Given the absence of a global drugs squad or any world organization with the authority to impose and implement measures to combat the illicit trade in narcotics, any effective policy ultimately has to depend upon voluntary co-operation between national governments, with them each agreeing to implement internationally agreed measures within their own territory. Although the United Nations International Drug Control Programme (UNDCP) is responsible for co-ordinating the implementation of international policies to combat the illegal drugs trade, it has no power to ensure compliance. Likewise, the G8 member states rely solely upon their domestic agencies, such as the US Drug Enforcement Agency and Her Majesty's Customs and Exercise, to enforce international initiatives. Since governments, along with their drug enforcement agencies, tend to have their own national priorities and seldom willingly relinquish any control over domestic matters, the result is a haphazard and largely incoherent global drugs control programme. As a consequence, organized crime tends to concentrate its drugs money laundering operations '... in countries where enforcement is weak and legislation absent or embryonic' (UNDCP, 1997, p.141). This serves to underline the crucial difference between the domestic and international spheres. In the latter, there is no world government akin to national government to ensure compliance with internationally agreed anti-drug policies or adherence to international treaties prohibiting the production and trafficking of illicit drugs. As the UNDCP report notes, 'The operation of the international drug control system is based on the principles of national control by States as well as international cooperation between States' (UNDCP, 1997 p.168).

Despite its antiquity, the norms, principles and practices of the Westphalian system continue to influence the governance of contemporary global affairs, as the case of controlling illegal narcotics illustrates. Furthermore, these principles and practices reinforce the perceived dichotomy between domestic and international affairs: the domestic realm is defined by the existence of government – the central institution of political rule – and the international realm by its evident absence. Accordingly, the Westphalian system embodies a conception of political space as largely coterminous with national territorial boundaries, reflecting a 'state as container' view of politics and social life. Among inter-nationalists, the Westphalian system remains central to the constitution of modern political life and to understanding the nature and dynamics of how the world is governed today. For globalists and transformationalists, the Westphalian Ideal seems to be at odds with the expanding scale upon which contemporary economic, cultural and political activity is currently organized. This challenge demands further investigation.

2.2 Political globalization: the emergence of global politics

Britain today is deeply enmeshed in regional and global institutions and networks, from the EU to global money laundering. Transnational connections and flows have developed within virtually all areas of human activity and, with the explosive growth of the Internet, within the realm of virtual reality too. Goods, capital, knowledge, ideas and weapons, as well as crime, pollutants, fashions and micro-organisms readily move across national territorial boundaries. Every month, the New York Public Library reports 10 million information requests from across the globe on its main web site, compared to 50,000 books dispensed to its local users (Darnton, 1999, p.371). Far from nation-states being 'discrete power containers' they have become more akin to 'a space of flows', that is, spaces permeated and transgressed by global and transnational flows and networks (see Figure 4.9 on page 149). Moreover, the regional and global scale on which many aspects of contemporary social and economic activity is organized, whether it is the illegal drugs trade (see Figure 4.4 overleaf) or the production of automobiles (as in Figure 1.11 in Chapter 1), links together the fate of communities in disparate regions of the globe in complex ways. As Sandel observes, under conditions of globalization, modern states: '... traditionally the vehicles of self-government ... find themselves increasingly unable to bring their citizens' judgements and values to bear on the economic forces that govern their destinies' (Sandel, 1996, p.339).

The globalists and transformationalists argue that power is no longer primarily organized and exercised on a national scale but, increasingly, has acquired a transnational, regional or even global dimension. As a consequence, the business of government and politics, itself, is becoming internationalized and globalized.

2.2.1 The internationalization of the state

At the 1998 G8 Birmingham Summit, the leaders of the world's most powerful governments came together to discuss a range of global issues that affected them all. The agenda ranged from the reform of the global financial architecture, following the East Asian economic crash in 1997, to the global drugs trade.

At this summit, the leaders of the G8 countries agreed to an ambitious action plan to co-ordinate their national programmes and policies with respect to combating the linked threats of illegal drugs trafficking and organized crime (Hajnal, 1999, p.3). Subsequently, the UN General Assembly announced a new war on illicit drugs, including a new convention against transnational organized crime. As the UN Secretary General noted, 'Alas, no country can hope to stem the drugs trade but together the world can' (UN Chronicle, 1998).

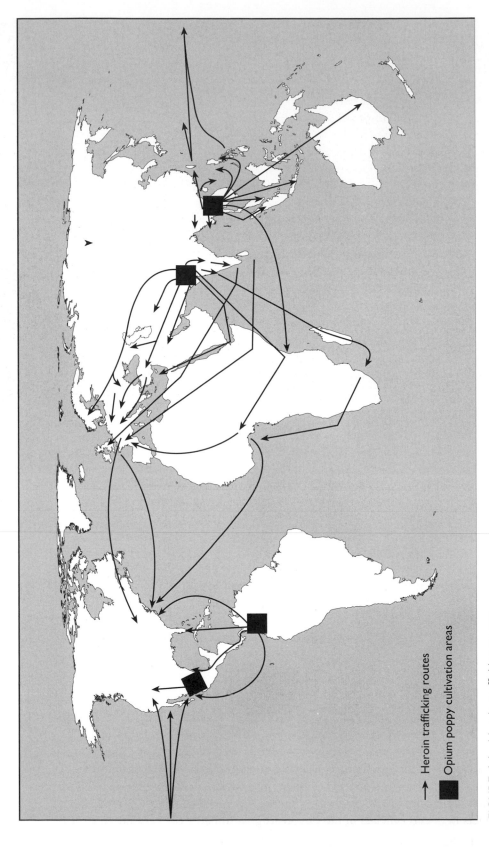

FIGURE 4.4 Heroin trafficking routes
Source: UNDCP, 1997

→ Heroin trafficking routes

■ Opium poppy cultivation areas

FIGURE 4.5   G8 Birmingham Summit, 1998

In the G8, responsibility for monitoring and advancing these initiatives lies with its Senior Experts Group on Transnational Organized Crime (Lyon Group), while within the UN it is the responsibility of the UNDCP. Behind these two bodies, routine co-operation between national drug enforcement agencies and police forces, through Interpol and regional agencies, such as Europol, the Inter-American Drug Abuse Control Commission and the Central Asian Republics' Drug Programme, constitutes a significant internationalization of governmental efforts to prevent or regulate the illegal drugs trade. This internationalization of the state, however, is not simply confined to obvious trans-border problems, such as drugs, but applies to almost every aspect of the business of government, from matters of social security and taxation, to the environment and food safety standards. Over the last fifty years there has been a dramatic internationalization of government activities as politicians try to control or re-regulate those activities and problems which, increasingly, escape national jurisdiction or which have their roots abroad.

This internationalization of the state is evident at a number of levels. Almost every Whitehall department has its own international office which deals directly, and often with little central co-ordination, with official counterparts in foreign governments, the EU or those international organizations to which the UK is affiliated. In addition to Whitehall's contact, the growth of direct contacts between officials in the devolved governments of Scotland and

Wales, and at local government level, not only with counterparts in the EU but also other local and regional governments in Europe, further complicates the picture. At the European level, institutions like the European Commission formalize and institutionalize co-operation between national governments that are closely connected by ties of history and geography.

At the global level there has been an explosive growth in the number of intergovernmental organizations (IGOs) – from 37 in 1909 to almost 300 in 1999 – whose activities mirror the functional responsibilities of national government departments, embracing everything from finance to flora and fauna. In addition to formal organizations such as the International Monetary Fund (IMF) and the World Health Organization (WHO), a multiplicity of high-level working groups of officials, summits, conferences and congresses and much informal contact and co-ordination exists. A century ago, few international summits were held; today there are in excess of 4,000 annually.

So extensive is this activity that the Foreign Office has no precise idea of how many international organizations, congresses and summits the British government participates in annually. With the internationalization of the state, the central organs of government, such as the British Cabinet, can barely monitor the plethora of trans or inter-governmental activity, let alone directly control it.

2.2.2 The transnationalization of political activity

Transnationalization
The growth of contacts, networks and organizations which link people, business and communities across national boundaries.

If globalization has been associated with the internationalization of the state, it has also facilitated and encouraged a corresponding **transnationalization** of politics, that is, activity which transcends or cuts across societies. In drugs prevention and control, hundreds of non-governmental organizations (NGOs) from across the globe, working in areas as diverse as drug education, rural development and child welfare, regularly come together at UN-sponsored conferences. Here they not only promote closer transnational co-operation in the struggle against the illicit drugs trade but also attempt to shape the direction of global policy on drugs. For the political debate about narcotics – prohibition versus liberalization, prevention versus regulation, legal versus voluntary control – cuts across national frontiers.

By mobilizing and organizing common interests across frontiers, NGOs seek to shape not only the anti-drug policies of regional and global bodies, such as the EU and the UNDCP, but also their own national governments. But the same infrastructures that facilitate transnational co-operation and communication among agents of civil society, such as Greenpeace or the worldwide Women's Movement, also enable transnational networking among the agencies of 'uncivil' society, namely organized crime and racist or terrorist movements. In the same way that NGOs gather to debate a global drugs policy, a less well documented diplomacy between the representatives of organized crime (the Cosa Nostra, the Russian Mafia, Triads and Yakuza) has developed in the form of global drugs cartels (Booth, 1996).

FIGURE 4.6 Kenyan NGO involved in preventive education about drugs

Over recent decades, there has been a surge in the numbers of transnational organizations, movements and networks which bring together and mobilize communities of interest, expertise or belief across national frontiers. From the World Development Movement to the World Muslim Congress, the Annual International Father Christmas Congress to the World Police and Fire Games, the Beijing Women's Forum to the Jubilee 2000 campaign, the International Accounting Standards Committee to the International Political Science Association, people are increasingly organizing and mobilizing, with the assistance of the Internet, across territories and continents in the pursuit of particular or universal interests, beliefs, causes or professional purposes.

At the start of the twentieth century, a few hundred transnational (i.e. non-governmental) organizations were officially recognized; at the start of the twenty-first century the number exceeded 5,000 (see Figure 4.7 overleaf). Despite difficulties in establishing reliable statistics about NGOs, the trend nevertheless points to the growing significance of transnational political connections and organizations in co-ordinating resources, information and power across societies. This is as evident in the temporary campaigns, such as the campaign to ban landmines popularized by Princess Diana, to the more permanent coalitions between international unions and human rights activists seeking the implementation of the worldwide ban on child labour.

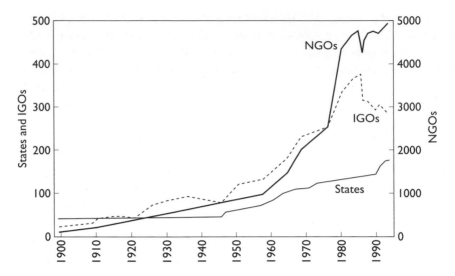

FIGURE 4.7   Growth of intergovernmental organizations (IGOs) and non-governmental organizations (NGOs) since 1900
Source: Held *et al.*, 1999, p.151

2.2.3   So what's new?

Although, as inter-nationalists correctly observe, the era of global empires in the late nineteenth century involved both the internationalization of the metropolitan states, through, for instance, the imposition of rule from Whitehall, and the transnationalization of political activity, as in the global campaign to abolish slavery, political globalization today is marked by a number of distinctive features.

1   There has been a remarkable institutionalization of intergovernmental and transnational networks of political interaction. This is expressed in, among other things, the establishment of formal organizations, such as the UN and Greenpeace, and more informal bodies, such as regular contacts between the central bankers of the world's most powerful states and the existence of transnational drug cartels.

2   The growth of new centres of authority above, below and alongside the state. So, for instance, in the UK, government in Whitehall (and hence British citizens) may be subject to the actions of bodies including, among others, the World Trade Organization (WTO), the EU, the Welsh and Scottish Assemblies and foreign multinational corporations.

3   The emergence of a fragile but nonetheless evolving global polity. Although no world government exists (or is ever likely to) the multiplicity of global and regional bodies that have been created to deal with matters that cut across national borders – such as the UNDCP and the EU – constitute a nascent system of global (and regional) governance. Global governance refers to a process of political co-ordination among governments, intergovernmental and transnational agencies (both public and private). It works towards common purposes or collectively agreed

goals, through making or implementing global or transnational rules, and managing trans-border problems. It differs dramatically from a concept of world government that presupposes the idea of one central global public authority legislating for humanity. Instead, the notion of global governance refers to the process by which individual governments, inter-governmental bodies (such as the UN), NGOs and transnational organizations, from the World Wildlife Fund to the Monsanto Corporation, come together to establish global rules, norms and standards or to regulate or resolve specific trans-border problems, such as the global drugs trade. But this does not mean that all governments or groups have an equal input into global decision making. On the contrary, great inequalities of power, access and influence exist. Global terrorist organizations such as al-Qaida can be seen as arising from such power imbalances.

4 Alongside this global polity is a developing infrastructure of transnational civil society. The plethora of NGOs, transnational organizations (from the International Chamber of Commerce to the Catholic Church), advocacy networks (from the Women's Movement to 'Nazis on the Net') and citizens' groups play a significant role in mobilizing, organizing, and exercising people-power across national boundaries. This has been facilitated by the speed and ease of modern global communications and the growing awareness of common interests between people in different countries and regions of the world. This explosion of 'citizen diplomacy' constitutes a rudimentary **transnational civil society**, in other words, a political arena in which citizens and private interests collaborate across borders to advance their mutual goals or to bring governments and the formal institutions of global governance to account for their activities.

Transnational civil society
The collective activities of all non-governmental organizations in global politics.

Although the idea of transnational civil society presumes and builds upon an important distinction concerning relations between states and relations between peoples, conceptually, the two cannot be readily divorced. In recent years, many of the key institutions of global and regional governance, from the UN to the EU, have encouraged the participation and representation of the 'ambassadors' of transnational civil society in their formal or informal deliberations. At the UN Earth Summit in Rio in 1992, for example, the formal representatives of government were outnumbered by the key representatives of environmental, corporate and other interested parties.

Of course, not all the members of transnational civil society are either civil or representative; while some seek to further dubious or anti-social causes, many lack effective accountability. Furthermore, there are considerable inequalities between the members of transnational civil society in terms of resources, influence and access to the key centres of decision making. Multinational corporations, such as Murdoch's News International, have much greater access to centres of power and a greater capacity to shape the global agenda than does, for example, the Rainforest Action Network. And not all interests are organized, so many of the poorest and most vulnerable members of the world community have no effective voice at all.

5   The existence of a system of global governance and transnational civil society is associated with new forms of multinational, transnational and global politics. Within the EU, for instance, the British government can be outvoted on certain issues, while trade rules within the WTO are equally binding on all governments and can be enforced by trade sanctions against those refusing to adhere to them. The national interest is often substantially redefined by participation in international organizations, as governments become socialized into broader collective aims. Thus, for instance, Britain's national defence policy has become indistinguishable from that of NATO's. Beyond governments, the existence of the Internet allows citizens' groups and social movements to mobilize and co-ordinate public opinion and protest across national frontiers with relative speed and ease, as was illustrated by the demonstrators at the WTO negotiations in Seattle in 1999. Under conditions of contemporary globalization, the organization and exercise of political power and protest is no longer simply a national or local affair.

Governments, and their citizens, have become embedded in more expansive networks and layers of regional and global governance. Indeed, the form and intensity of contemporary political globalization poses profound challenges to the 'states as containers' view of political life since it challenges the basic assumptions of the Westphalian conception of the world. In particular, transformationalists argue, political space is no longer coterminous with national territory and national governments are no longer the sole masters of their own or their citizens' fate. But this does not mean that national governments or national politics have been eclipsed by the forces of economic, cultural and political globalization. Nation-states still wage war, as we saw in the war against Iraq in 2003, but in some cases, as after the 11 September 2001 attacks on New York and Washington, the 'enemy' is not a single nation-state. The state is not in decline, as many globalists suggest, but its power and authority are being reconfigured in the context of a multi-layered system of global governance.

2.3   The infrastructure of global governance

Since the end of the Cold War, the existing system of global governance has acquired an almost universal reach such that few domains of global activity and few countries are outside its jurisdiction. Building upon the institutions and frameworks of co-operation established in the aftermath of the Second World War, the infrastructure of global governance has evolved into a complex and multi-layered system which has no single centre of authority. Accordingly, it is often described as *pluralistic* since it depends on a multiplicity of agencies – from states and governmental organizations to multinational corporations – coming together to agree global rules, norms or policies. One way to view this system is as three distinctive layers or infrastructures of governance: the suprastate; the substate; and the transnational (Scholte, 1997). Sandwiched between these three layers is the national government layer.

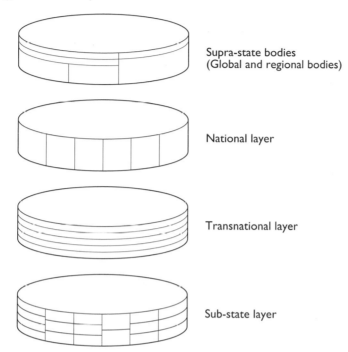

Supra-state bodies
(Global and regional bodies)

National layer

Transnational layer

Sub-state layer

FIGURE 4.8 Multi-layered global governance – the 'layer cake' model

Source: Adapted from Modelski, 1972

Each of these layers, both separately and in conjunction, constitutes a framework within which governments and peoples seek to engage with the global and local conditions which shape their fate and to bring to account the exercise of power. Let's examine this 'layer cake' model of global governance in a little more detail.

2.3.1 The suprastate layer

In the last fifty years there has been a phenomenal expansion in the number, jurisdiction and global impact of inter-governmental organizations; that is, international bodies brought into being by formal agreements between governments. What distinguishes the major intergovernmental organizations from more informal co-operative arrangements is usually that the former have a cafeteria and a pension scheme; namely, they have some kind of autonomous legal personality. Moreover, membership of such organizations has been increasing such that most now have almost universal coverage. Although a few existing international organizations, such as the International Telecommunications Organization, date back to the nineteenth century, and some, such as the International Labour Organization (ILO), have their origins in the aftermath of the First World War, by far the largest number – well over 250 – have been created since 1945. While the majority of organizations have functional responsibility for a particular sector of global activity – for example the International Civil Aviation Organization concerns itself with air transportation matters – others, such as the UN and the Organization for Security and Co-operation in Europe, have more wide-ranging responsibilities.

In addition to these functional and universal bodies, the last two decades of the twentieth century witnessed a remarkable growth in the emergence of regional groupings and organizations on every single continent (see Table 4.1).

TABLE 4.1 Regional groupings formed since 1980

	Acronym	Date of Formation
Organization of East Caribbean States	OECS	1981
Gulf Co-operation Council	GCC	1982
Economic Community of West African States	ECOWAS	1983
South Asian Association for Regional Co-operation	SAARC	1985
Arab Maghreb Union	AMU	1989
Asia-Pacific Economic Co-operation	APEC	1989
Latin American Integration Association	ALADI	1990
Visegrad group		1991
South African Development Community	SADC	1992
Common Market for East and Southern Africa	COMESA	1993
Association of Caribbean States	ACS	1994
Group of 3 – Colombia, Mexico, Venezuela		1994
North American Free Trade Agreement	NAFTA	1994
Economic and Monetary Community of Central Africa	CEMAC	1994
Union economique et monetaire ouest-africaine	UEMOA	1994
South American Common Market	MERCOSUR	1995

Source: Adapted from Elazar, 1998, pp.359

Just as the EU has deepened the process of integration among its member states, parallel developments are occurring in other regions, although at a much slower pace and according to a more restrictive vision of regional integration. While the emphasis in NAFTA, APEC and MERCOSUR is upon negative integration – removing barriers which prevent or slow down trade and co-operation between member states – rather than building institutions for collective decision making, nevertheless, regional governance arrangements are becoming more entrenched features of the global political landscape. Indeed, recent years have witnessed the emergence of inter-regional diplomacy as regional blocs seek to build global alliances and preferential arrangements with each other – much like the global alliances forged between partner airlines in the late 1990s.

In seeking to give some strategic direction to this proliferation of suprastate activity, governmental leaders have resorted to summitry i.e. formal meetings between heads of government. In general, summits, such as the G8 and the European Council (comprising the heads of EU governments) have become more frequent, more institutionalized and more substantive. The G8 is often regarded as a kind of 'global directorate' since it brings together the leaders of the world's most economically (and militarily) powerful states whose collective decisions or veto can have a critical influence on the global agenda and the politics of global governance. The G8's decision at the Cologne Summit in June 1999 to waive much of the debt of the world's poorest indebted countries is indicative of its capacity to act decisively, even when such action is opposed by powerful forces within G8 member governments.

The influence of suprastate governance has been experienced in the UK in several ways. As the jurisdiction of the EU and international organizations has expanded, more aspects of domestic and local public policy have suddenly acquired a European or global dimension. On issues ranging from corporal punishment in schools to the war on illegal drugs, the international community – in the form of the European Court and the UNDCP respectively – has acquired a voice in the making of public policy. Alongside the widening jurisdiction of suprastate bodies has come the deepening impact of the policies of institutions, such as the WTO, on UK citizens. In the case of the WTO, whose primary function is to reduce national barriers to trade, matters such as local health and safety standards can be questioned if these appear to give an unfair competitive advantage to domestic over foreign producers. Given the enormous range and number of suprastate bodies to which the UK government belongs, it has become increasingly difficult for the central organs of government to monitor, let alone give coherence to, the various positions adopted by the many government departments which now represent the UK in these diverse forums. Indeed, within the EU especially, strong transgovernmental policy networks or policy communities have evolved such that major conflicts of interest no longer necessarily divide along national lines but rather along functional or departmental lines. Thus it is not unusual to witness EU finance ministers, including the Chancellor of the Exchequer, in conflict with EU agriculture ministers, including the British Minister for Agriculture, over the budget of the Common Agricultural Policy. Rather than speaking with a single voice to the world – the national interest – the British state often can be likened to a Mozart opera in which, to rather enchanting effect, the leading players sing in harmony but entirely different tunes and lyrics. In other words, the growth of suprastate bodies has encouraged such a fragmentation of central government that the British state no longer always appears as a unified actor on the global scene and sometimes fails to project a coherent national interest. This sense of fragmentation is reinforced by the growth of substate networks and structures of governance.

2.3.2 The substate layer

Recent years have witnessed a substantial expansion in the role of local governments and substate authorities in the global arena, as they seek to promote the cultural, economic and political interests of their locale. As global competition to attract foreign investment has intensified, cities, regions and sub-national authorities have become increasingly active at global and regional levels. This activism takes a number of forms: from establishing local diplomatic missions abroad, through representation in key global and regional forums, to the creation of formal bodies, such as the International Union of Local Authorities. Through such mechanisms, substate governments can take significant policy initiatives which, in many cases, may bypass their own central government. They also provide a framework within which collaborative initiatives to deal with common or shared problems, from the illegal drugs trade to environmental pollution, can be pursued.

Many UK local authorities (e.g. Coventry) maintain their own representatives in Brussels while, through the EU's Committee of the Regions, regional governments, including that of Scotland, have a major input into policy deliberations on European-wide issues which have significant regional impacts. Substate authorities also have acquired an important role in implementing many globally-agreed norms and measures. Glasgow City Council, for example, has taken many initiatives on local environmental policies in accordance with Agenda 21, agreed at the UN Earth Summit in Rio in 1992. The Foreign Office may still be the official voice of British interests in Europe and the wider world, but it is no longer the sole expression of those interests. The representatives of devolved governments in Edinburgh, Cardiff and Belfast, and many municipal authorities such as Manchester and Coventry, increasingly seek to create their own distinctive international identity. Whitehall no longer has a monopoly on how local communities engage with Europe or the wider world but neither do public authorities.

2.3.3 The transnational layer

Whereas, for much of this century, international diplomacy was essentially an activity in which only consenting states could engage, the growth of suprastate organizations, such as the UN or the WTO, has created new arenas in which the voice of peoples – as opposed to governments – is increasingly heard. Most intergovernmental organizations have encouraged NGOs and transnational movements to participate directly or indirectly in their deliberations as a way to legitimize their authority or to acquire much needed expertise. Even the WTO and the World Bank, among the most secretive of international bodies, have been forced (under public pressure) to become more open to the representatives of transnational civil society. Accordingly, some argue that the global communications revolution has been accompanied by a global associational revolution, as citizens, communities and private interests have organized to influence the conduct and content of global governance (Rosenau, 1990). Across the entire spectrum of public issues, from the ecological to the ecumenical, NGOs and transnational movements give expression to the concerns and interests of an emerging transnational civil society.

The power and influence of transnational movements arises from their capacity to organize people and resources across national frontiers in the pursuit of collective goals. Since there is a great diversity of transnational movements – from large and well-organized groups, such as Greenpeace, to more spontaneous groups, such as the Women Living Under Muslim Laws Network – it is difficult to generalize about their power and political impact. For the most part, however, many transnational movements and NGOs lack the kind of economic, financial or political resources that states and multinational companies can draw upon. Accordingly, their influence and political impact is best measured not in terms of raw power capabilities, which tend to be limited, but, rather, in terms of infrastructural power.

This infrastructural power is manifest in the political strategies through which transnational movements and organizations gain a voice in global governance. They tend to exert influence by:

- shaping public attitudes, interests and identities
- altering the agenda of local, national and global politics
- providing communities and citizens with a channel of access to global and regional decision-making forums
- exercising moral, spiritual or technical authority
- seeking to make governments, international bodies and corporate empires accountable for their actions and decisions.

Take, for instance, Amnesty International as an example of a well-known transnational social movement. By mobilizing people across the globe it has raised public consciousness of human rights and contributed to the creation of a global political culture of rights. More tangibly – through public campaigns, access to the Foreign Office and the UN and its many functional agencies such as the ILO – bodies like Amnesty International help define the global agenda by ensuring that the issue of human rights is not conveniently forgotten. Aside from agenda setting, Amnesty International also provides an institutional mechanism, outside the direct control of the British or any other national government, through which individuals can participate in global affairs. This takes many forms, from letter writing campaigns to protesting against specific human rights abuses. In certain contexts, bodies like Amnesty International may also exercise considerable independent authority. In advocating particular causes and defending universal norms, they exert a certain moral authority in global affairs. In addition, their expertise and experience in human rights law endows them with considerable technical authority. In the case of Amnesty International, regularly published bulletins of human rights abuses perpetrated by governments on their own citizens or citizens of other countries are central to the creation of a global system and culture of accountability of states to peoples.

Of course, not all transnational movements and NGOs are as well resourced as Amnesty International, nor do all the world's peoples have an equal opportunity to participate in this way in global affairs. Inequalities of power within transnational civil society are much more decidedly marked than those within UK society. Not only are there inequalities between different regions of the world – Africa, for instance, is home to few transnational movements or NGOs with a global influence – but these are often compounded by economic, gender, information and ethnic inequalities which transcend national borders. Diverse as it is, transnational civil society remains decidedly unrepresentative of the world's peoples.

Among the most visible and powerful constituencies in transnational civil society are those representing the interests of global corporate empires, global capital and business interests. In 1997, for instance, the world sales of General Motors amounted to almost double the national income of the Philippines, while the national income of Greece was less than the world sales of either Mitsubishi or the Royal Dutch Shell Group (UNDP, 1999, p.32). With enormous resources at their disposal, and given that most governments and governmental agencies are obsessed by the imperatives of economic growth, multinational corporations and the plethora of transnational business associations that have grown up to represent corporate interests – for example, the World Business Council – have acquired a privileged position in the governance of the global economy. But their influence extends well beyond the economic domain since few issues, whether global warming or human rights in Chile, can be divorced from economic interests or calculations.

2.4 Global politics: the transformationalist case

Rather than the 'state as container' metaphor, transformationalists suggest that a much more accurate metaphor for a globalizing world would be the 'state as a space of flows' (see Figure 4.9). The internationalization of government activity and the transnationalization of societies imply that power and politics flow through, across and around territorial boundaries. Political activity and the business of governing have become stretched across frontiers such that a distinctive form of global politics is emerging.

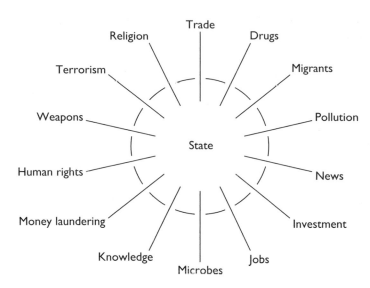

FIGURE 4.9   The state as a space of flows
Source: Adapted from Scholte, 1997

According to transformationalists, the notion of global politics does not deny the continuing significance of national politics or politics between states, i.e. traditional geo-politics, but it does suggest that both are embedded in a dense web of social, economic and political relations which transcend national borders, in turn creating overlapping, rather than territorially exclusive **communities of fate**. In the 'global neighbourhood' all politics, understood as the pursuit of power and justice, is ultimately global politics.

Communities of fate
Social groups/ collectivities that share a common destiny or sense of solidarity.

SUMMARY

- Transformationalists argue that the emergence of global politics does not imply the end of the state but, rather, the reconfiguration of state power.

- Global politics acknowledges the existence of overlapping communities of fate and the significance of multi-layered global governance in the management of human affairs.

3 GOVERNING THE GLOBAL NEIGHBOURHOOD

Besides initiatives to combat the illegal drugs trade, the 1998 G8 Birmingham Summit announced important measures to reform the governance of international finance. In 1997, speculators on global financial markets had triggered a severe devaluation of the Thai baht which, in turn, undermined investor confidence in other East Asian economies and culminated in the worst economic crisis to afflict the region since the 1930s. The East Asian crash threatened to de-stabilize the international financial system and tip the entire world towards recession. Many City-based banks and investment funds were significantly exposed to the mounting economic crisis in East Asia, while in Wales and the North East, communities watched anxiously as jobs disappeared overnight when Korean and Japanese firms cut back plans for European expansion. The same story was replicated in other countries in Europe and the Americas. The US President referred to it as the most serious global financial crisis since the 1930s. In an effort to prevent a global recession, the major economic powers – the US, Germany, Japan and Britain – co-ordinated their policy responses and funded, through the IMF and the World Bank, the largest multilateral financial rescue package in post-Second World War history. At Birmingham they sought agreement on how to tame the power of global financial markets.

For transformationalists, the East Asian crisis is indicative of the extent to which globalization has resulted in a shifting balance of power between states and global markets. They also argue that it demonstrates the centrality of global economic governance to ensuring the stability of the world economy. Hugely significant decisions were taken by the IMF, multinational banks and investment funds in New York, London and elsewhere. These had dramatic implications for the economic security and well-being of entire nations, communities and households across the globe – from the value of our pension funds and the jobs of workers in South Wales, to the collapse of Mr Salamet's rickshaw business in Mojokerto (400 miles east of Jakarta). As a result of the financial crisis, Mr Salamet was forced to witness the agonising death of his mother because he was unable to afford the prescribed pain-killers, and watch his children go hungry (Kristof and Wyatt, 1999).

FIGURE 4.10   Mr Salamet: a victim of the East Asian crash

Indeed the management of the East Asian financial crisis raises fundamental questions about the form of global governance today, especially its democratic credentials. In whose interests does the existing system of global governance function? How is the business of global governance conducted? How are global rules made and implemented? To what extent is the system accountable and to whom? Where does power lie?

In seeking to address these questions we need to draw upon existing theories of global governance. The study of global politics has generated three distinctive accounts of global governance and we will examine each briefly in turn. These three accounts are referred to here as: inter-nationalist, globalist and transformationalist.

ACTIVITY 4.2

To consolidate your understanding of each of these accounts, complete the relevant column of the summary grid below as you study each of the subsequent sections.

TABLE 4.2 Theories of global governance: summary grid

	Inter-nationalist	Globalist	Transformationalist
Key agents/ agencies of rule			
Who rules?			
In whose interest?			
Through what means?			
To what ends?			

3.1 Hegemonic governance – the inter-nationalist argument

At the height of the East Asian financial crisis in late 1997, the US Treasury and the White House vetoed a Japanese government initiative to establish a regional fund, to be administered collectively by East Asian governments. The fund was to have provided financial assistance to countries like South Korea that had been hardest hit by the crash. This proposal was unacceptable to the US since it feared such a regionally-based fund would shy away from imposing vital economic and financial reforms upon the recipients of aid. Instead, with the assistance of the IMF, the US Treasury engineered the largest multilateral financial rescue package – in excess of $116 billion – since the Marshall Plan aid to Europe after the Second World War (Godement, 1999). This despite the fact that the banks most exposed to the rising tide of East Asian debt were all European rather than American. Moreover, fearful of the crash enveloping the rest of the world, the US Federal Reserve (the equivalent of the Bank of England) took corrective action. It cut US domestic interest rates which boosted the world economy and reduced the possibility of a downward spiral into global recession. Because the US is the single largest economy in the world and the pre-eminent – hegemonic – global power, its role in managing the East Asian financial crisis was decisive.

Hegemonic governance
Government by the great power(s) of the day.

As a contemporary illustration of the inter-nationalist theory of **hegemonic governance**, the US management of the East Asian crisis through 1997–8 is almost unique. Central to the inter-nationalist account is an emphasis upon the structure of power in the inter-state system and, in particular, the way in which the hierarchy of power determines the pattern of global governance. During the Cold War, when the USSR and the US were locked into a contest for global hegemony, the pattern of global governance was very different from that of today. As the agreement of both was necessary for any effective global action to occur and since that agreement was rarely forthcoming on the most critical issues confronting the world community, the UN and many of the institutions of global governance experienced effective political paralysis. In the post-Cold War era, the US has emerged as the only global superpower and, although it remains unwilling to devote either the resources or the attention to running the world, it does, nevertheless, have a critical veto over most aspects of global governance. As the inter-nationalist theory of hegemonic governance suggests, it is not that the great powers, such as the US, legislate for the rest of the world or directly control the institutions of global governance, but, rather, their capacity to veto or bypass international bodies, such as the UN, gives them enormous influence over the management of global affairs.

To summarize, the inter-nationalist theory of hegemonic governance emphasizes the crucial significance of the dominant power(s) of the day in shaping the structures, patterns and outcomes of global governance. Moreover, it implies, contrary to much popular belief, that processes of globalization are not, as many globalists assert, out of control but are the product of a US-inspired liberal world order. To this extent, globalization is conceived as being synonymous with Americanization, that is, the extension of American culture, political power and liberal capitalism.

3.2 Global Capital Rules OK! – the globalist argument

In his book *One World, Ready or Not*, William Greider argues that as capitalism has become globalized even the most powerful states, such as the US, find themselves engulfed by the imperatives of the global market (Greider, 1997). Rather than conceiving hegemony in statist terms – the primacy of the US as the only global superpower – more radical globalist accounts stress the hegemony of global corporate capital and the consolidation, over recent decades, of a new form of global capitalist order. In this account, the infrastructure of global governance is in the grip of powerful transnational social forces – elite, corporate and bureaucratic networks – which is centred on the US, but whose wealth, power and privileges are bound up with the reproduction and expansion of global corporate capitalism. So, even though few American banks were at risk in the East Asian crisis, the US Treasury and the IMF acted promptly in order to stabilize the global financial system. Furthermore, the economic reforms imposed by the IMF on several East Asian countries, in return for much needed loans, have created new opportunities for consolidating the power of global capital across the region, for example through mergers such as Renault with Nissan, and through rationalization.

Underlying this radical account is a conception of world order in which global capitalism is considered to have primacy; a conception in which political empires have been replaced by corporate empires. The conduct and content of global governance is shaped by an unwritten constitution which automatically privileges the interests and agenda of global capital, often at the expense of the welfare of nations, communities and the natural environment. In effect, the institutions of global governance and the apparatus of nation-states are effectively transmission belts for securing and managing the global capitalist order in accordance with the disciplines of global markets and the imperative of global accumulation, that is, profit seeking.

A globalist interpretation of the East Asian crash would identify the significance of transnational elite networks among politicians, finance ministers, central bankers, bureaucratic, corporate and multilateral bodies (a **cosmocracy**) in co-operating to defuse and resolve the crisis before it threatened the stability of the global financial system or tipped the world into recession. In sum: the existing system of global governance provides a structure for nurturing, legitimizing and protecting the global capitalist order.

Cosmocracy
A global capitalist elite.

3.3 People power – the transformationalist argument

While the transformationalist account recognizes the importance of the dominant powers and global capital to any understanding of global governance, it dismisses the determinism of both the inter-nationalist and the globalist accounts. Transformationalists believe that both these accounts overemphasize structure at the expense of agency. The transformationalist account seeks to acknowledge the significance of both the changing structure or context of politics and governance, brought about by globalization, *and* the importance of political agents in shaping the conduct and content of global governance. In this sense, it emphasizes reflexivity rather than determinism. In so doing, it tends to stress the importance of people power and the role of expertise in making sense of global governance.

It would be facile to argue, nor do all advocates of the globalist account, that the institutions of global governance simply constitute an 'executive committee of the [global] bourgeoisie'. The terms of economic globalization have always been contested, from the campaigns against the Atlantic slave trade in the eighteenth century to Third World demands in the 1970s for a New International Economic Order. In recent decades the growing authority of regional and global institutions has created new arenas in which the terms of economic globalization have been, and continue to be, contested. In addition, the globalization of political activity has been accompanied by the emergence of a new kind of 'network politics' which, in mobilizing and organizing resistance to the rule of global capital, seeks to make global markets and global institutions work in the interests of the world's peoples rather than the other way round. This 'governance from below' represents an alternative politics of protest and transnational mobilization which has achieved some notable successes, one being the global 'Stop the MAI' campaign (see Box 4.1).

In some respects the global 'Stop the MAI' movement represents the first major campaign, using the Internet and network politics, to mobilize and organize transnational civil society successfully to challenge the imperatives of economic globalization. As one advocate of the MAI concluded:

> The fate of the MAI is a warning. Policy-makers need to prepare their ground far better than this. They also need to recognize the changed political context in which they operate. The enemies of the liberal international economy have found new arguments and new ways of organising. Both need to be resisted.
>
> (Wolf, 1999)

Governance from below, however, is likely to become a more, rather than less, significant channel through which communities and citizens hold the agencies of global governance to account for their actions. In the global neighbourhood, community politics has acquired a new impetus, as the

BOX 4.1   Case study: 'Stop the MAI' campaign

Room 2 in the basement in the Paris headquarters of the OECD – the club of mostly western, rich, industrial nations – was the location, between 1996 and 1999, of a series of virtually secret negotiations on a treaty to establish global rules for foreign investment, that is, rules governing international investment by multinational corporations. The Multilateral Agreement on Investment (MAI) began life as an EU proposal to complement the WTO's work in liberalizing trade by reducing barriers to investment by multinationals. Its political significance was recognized by the then Director General of the WTO who referred to the MAI as '...writing the constitution of a single global economy' (Barlow and Clarke, 1998, p.33). This was no exaggeration in the sense that the MAI set out to establish a 'bill of rights' for foreign multinational corporations operating abroad, thus, by default, redefining the jurisdiction and authority of national governments in relation to multinationals. Such was the political sensitivity of the issues involved that it was not until well into the negotiations that the existence of the deliberations and a draft treaty was publicly acknowledged. This came about not from official sources but largely because of the global 'Stop the MAI' campaign.

The campaign was launched and co-ordinated by a number of environmental and labour NGOs from the major western states whom, among others from the international business community, OECD officials had sought to consult in the preparation of the draft treaty. By building national opposition to the MAI between like-minded labour, human rights, women's, environmental and community organizations, the 'Stop the MAI' campaign sought to co-ordinate these various national campaigns through groups such as the International Forum on Globalization. Its aim was to exacerbate divisions in the OECD negotiations and apply maximum public pressure where it was most politically effective. National petitions, demonstrations and protests against the MAI were organized so that in Australia and the US, Parliament and Congress respectively were forced to hold open public hearings. In the UK the 'Stop the MAI' campaign launched a national petition and lobbied MPs. Networking, through the use of the Internet, enabled strategic co-ordination of direct action and protest across many countries and among a diverse body of NGOs. By politicizing the MAI, the NGO-led campaign seized the initiative and sought to shift the agenda away from the issue of liberalization to the highly emotive matter of national economic sovereignty. With division growing within the OECD, and governments fearing a public backlash against the loss of sovereignty implied by the MAI, the negotiations collapsed and by early 1999 the draft treaty was placed in abeyance for the foreseeable future.

'Battle of Seattle' showed when, in December 1999, protesters expressed their opposition to the WTO. But governance by experts is also likely to be equally as significant.

Systemic risks
Collective dangers and threats created by global/regional activities.

Risk society
A society characterized by the perception of risks and dangers, which requires expert, specialist knowledge to deal with these perceived risks.

By creating global systems and networks of interaction – from global financial markets to the illegal drugs trade – globalization creates **systemic risks**, evident for instance in the threat of global financial meltdown posed by the events of the East Asian crash. Systemic risks harness the fate of communities in one region of the world to developments many thousands of miles away. In effect, globalization engenders a global '**risk society**'. In a risk society, many aspects of social life come to be governed by experts – those with specialist knowledge and experience – such that most of the routine aspects of global governance, as well as many critical ones, are the preserve of functional or expert bodies. Thus expert committees of the International Civil Aviation Organization legislate global norms for airline safety standards while the UNDCP regulates many of the technical aspects of the global war on illicit drugs. Indeed, regulating the illicit drugs trade is one area in which high risks and governance by experts – whether drug cartels or the World Customs Union – is much in evidence.

FIGURE 4.11   1909 Shanghai Conference: the first attempt to regulate the illegal drugs trade

Since the 1909 Shanghai Conference, when international co-operation to prevent the illegal drugs trade was inaugurated, experts in all aspects of the problem, from prevention to money laundering, have played a key role in defining and implementing global rules and programmes. While politicians and diplomats establish the broad principles of global regulation (such as the 1988 UN Convention against Illicit Traffic in Narcotic Drugs and Psychotropic Substances), most of the detailed negotiation and its implementation is the preserve of experts from law enforcement agencies to chemists tasked with defining 'illegal substances'. NGOs with expert knowledge, whether about rural development in the main producing countries or drug education and prevention matters, are also central to the regulatory process such that the number involved in the process has steadily increased (see Figure 4.12).

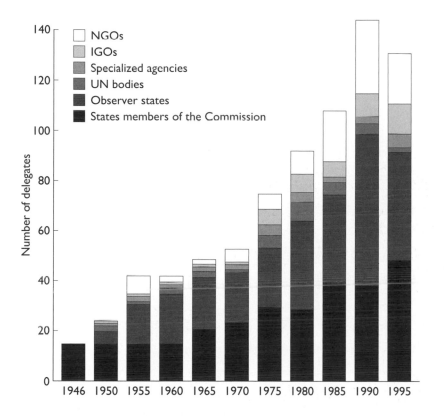

FIGURE 4.12
Attendance at sessions of the Commission on Narcotic Drugs
Source: UNDCP, 1997

Since the drugs issue cuts across so many aspects of public policy, from matters of health, education, policing, customs, law, banking and morality, it has increasingly become an arena in which experts and expertise tend to dominate. This, in many respects, is even the case in terms of the illegal drugs trade itself. Given that this industry '... carries a high penalty for inefficient risk management' (UNDCP, 1997, p.129), the narcotics trade has become a highly technical operation and is organized and managed on lines similar to that of a multinational firm (see Figure 4.13 overleaf).

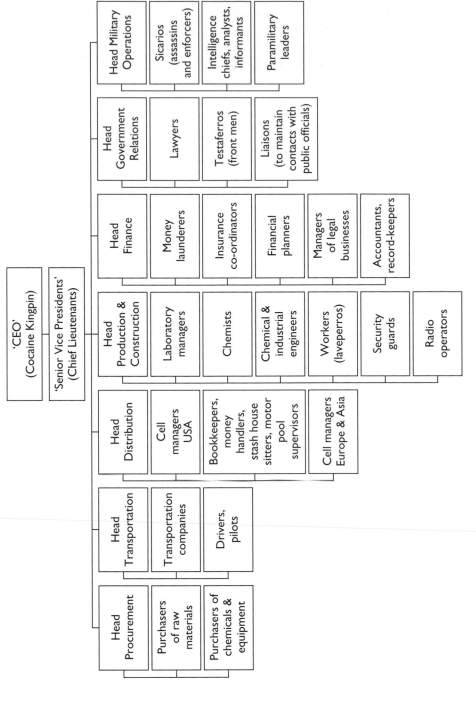

FIGURE 4.13 The cocaine trafficking organization as a corporation

Source: UNDCP, 1997

Since the illegal drugs trade is also cash intensive (American Express? No Thank You!) the laundering of drug money, for instance, has become a highly technical and technicized business. The 'laundromat' operation, as it is known, has its own technical codes and practices. These include pre-washing, placement, smurfing, layering and integration – the final stage at which the cash is returned to the business – which are organized on a worldwide scale to avoid detection (Booth, 1996, p.335).

In the realm of global drug control, a transnational community of experts exists which has a critical influence on how the international community deals with the question of drugs. The strength of this transnational – or epistemic (based on knowledge or expertise) – community is evident from the fact that despite poor diplomatic relations between the US and Iran, the drug agencies from both countries continue to co-operate in the 'war' against illegal narcotics. **Epistemic communities** de-politicize issues by redefining them as technical or procedural matters which are best resolved by experts. Expert knowledge and understanding become the primary credentials for participating in, and contributing to, the process of global governance. Decision making is thus legitimized by the application and interpretation of knowledge, technical rules and expertise. As Winner suggests, this kind of technocratic ethic means:

> ... the real voting will take place on a very high level of technical understanding. ... One may register to vote on this level only by exhibiting proper credentials as an expert. The balloting will be closed to the ignorant and to those whose knowledge is out of date or otherwise not relevant to the problem at hand. Among the disenfranchised in this arrangement are some previously formidable characters: the average citizen, the sovereign consumer ... and the home-grown politician.
>
> (Winner, 1997)

Epistemic community
A transnational network of experts.

Since the regulation of many global issue-areas, from the environment to the safety of air transport, has succumbed to the technocratic ethic, serious questions are posed about the democratic credentials of global governance.

ACTIVITY 4.3

At this point you might want to complete the final column of the summary grid that you started in Activity 4.2. When you have done this, compare it with my own attempt overleaf.

COMMENT

TABLE 4.3   Theories of global governance: summary grid

	Inter-nationalist (hegemonic governance)	Globalist (rule of global capital)	Transformationalist (technocratic governance, governance from below)
Key agents/ agencies of rule	Dominant states	Global corporate and financial capital	Epistemic communities, NGOs and social movements
Who rules?	Hierarchy – the US as hegemon	Cosmocracy – transnational business civilization	Polyarchy – diverse social forces and interests
In whose interests?	National and geo-strategic interests	Global capital	Sectional and collective People's and planetary interests
Through what means?	Coercion and consent	Structural power – global markets constrain what nation-states can do	Application of knowledge, procedures and technical deliberation Mobilization across borders, transnational coalition building
To what ends?	Maintenance of global order conducive to hegemonic interests	Stability and reproduction of global capitalist order	Efficient, accountable and effective governance Contesting and resisting globalization from above

For the transformationalists these three accounts of global governance are considered complementary rather than contradictory; each offers an insight into a particular dimension of global power relations. Indeed they correspond to the three principal structures that intersect to define the form of contemporary global governance and world order:

- geo-politics and the inter-state system
- the system of global capitalist production
- the global social system.

They relate the significance of state power, corporate power, and people power respectively to an understanding of how the world is governed, by whom, and in whose interests. Conceived in this complementary way, the transformationalist account acknowledges the strategic importance of the most powerful states and capitalist social forces, yet combines this with a critical appreciation of the multiple political forces which shape how the world is presently governed.

SUMMARY

- There are three accounts of global governance: inter-nationalist, globalist and transformationalist.
- The transformationalist account acknowledges the significance of hegemonic states and global capitalism in shaping the structures of global governance but considers both accounts as too determinist.
- The transformationalist account seeks to combine the insights of the inter-nationalist and globalist arguments with an emphasis upon governance from below and governance by experts.

4   POWER SHIFT: PUTTING NATIONAL GOVERNMENT IN ITS PLACE

● ●

Globalization, argue transformationalists, is contributing to a reconfiguration in the power and authority of national governments. Sovereignty, as British membership of the EU confirms, is no longer what it used to be; the Westphalian Ideal of statehood is being transformed. Some argue that we are now entering the era of post-sovereign governance (Scholte, 1997, p.72). But what exactly is the nature of this transformation and in what sense is state power being reconfigured?

ACTIVITY 4.4

At this point you might want to return to the earlier discussion of the principles of the Westphalian system in Section 2.1 and spend a few moments refreshing your memory of the five points noted there. Then complete the summary grid overleaf based upon what you understand the transformationalist argument to be.

The discussion below the grid should help you identify the main points of contention.

TABLE 4.4 Transformations in the Westphalian system

	Westphalian Ideal	Post-Westphalian system
Territoriality		
State sovereignty		
State autonomy		
Primacy		
Anarchy		

C O M M E N T

It is not part of the tranformationalist argument that national governments or the nation-state is in terminal decline or is being eclipsed by the forces of globalization. On the contrary, in some fundamental respects, from its capacity to raise taxes and revenues, intervene in its citizens' lives and threaten the nuclear obliteration of its enemies, the current British state is as powerful, if not more so, than its predecessors. Despite this, it is also the case that the demands upon the state have grown exponentially. Sandwiched between global, regional and local forces, government in Whitehall is having to adjust and redefine its roles and functions. In this respect, globalization involves a structural shift towards multi-layered global governance and so invites a corresponding adaptation of the state. This reconfiguration of state power is articulated in several ways.

- *Territoriality* The Westphalian system was based upon the principle of parcelling political space into discrete territorial chunks which became the basis for modern states. However, this conception of political space appears increasingly at odds with a world in which political power and authority is organized and exercised on a multiplicity of scales, from the local to the global. Borders and territory still remain important, not least for administrative purposes, but they have ceased to define the spatial markers of political life and political community. Under conditions of globalization, overlapping communities of fate and trans-border problems define a new geography of political community and political power.

- *State sovereignty* The sovereign power and authority of national government, i.e. the entitlement of states to rule within their own territorial space, is being redefined but not necessarily eroded. In the context of transnational systems of rule with other governments and agencies, states now use sovereignty less as a legal claim to supreme power than as a bargaining tool. Within this complex system of multi-layered governance, sovereignty is bartered, shared and divided among the agencies of public power at different levels. The Westphalian conception of sovereignty as an indivisible, territorially exclusive form of public power is being displaced by a new understanding of sovereignty as the shared exercise of public power and authority.

- *State autonomy* Far from globalization leading to 'the end of the state', it is bringing into being a more activist state. This is because, simply to achieve their domestic objectives, national governments are forced to engage in extensive multilateral collaboration and co-operation. But in becoming more embedded in frameworks of global and regional governance, states confront a real dilemma. In return for more effective public policy and meeting their citizens' demands, whether in relation to stopping the illegal drugs trade or creating employment, the state's capacity for self governance – that is, state autonomy – is compromised. On many issues, a difficult trade-off is posed between effective governance and self-governance.

- *Primacy* States no longer have a monopoly of authority over their citizens. The growth of new centres of public authority above and below the state, together with the emergence of private authorities, from multinational corporations to NGOs such as Amnesty International, have eroded the primacy of the state. Moreover, with the growth of transnational social movements and organizations, citizens' allegiances and identity are no longer exclusively defined by nationality or membership of the nation-state.

- *Anarchy* Rather than an anarchic world, in which there is no authority beyond the sovereign state, the contemporary world order might best be described as a **heterarchy**. Moreover, as the case of the illegal drugs trade shows, the distinction between the domestic and the international has been eroded as domestic matters have become internationalized and international affairs domesticated.

Heterarchy
A system in which political authority is shared and divided between different layers of governance and in which many agencies share in the task of governance.

The role, power, authority and function of national government is being transformed by globalization. A power shift is underway as political authority and power are diffused above, below and alongside the state. A new kind of state is slowly emerging and, with it, a new public philosophy of governance which recognizes the changed global context of political action. The command and control state of the Westphalian Ideal is being displaced by the

Reflexive state
Government by the strategic co-ordination of resources and networks of power from the global to the local.

reflexive or network state. The **reflexive state** seeks to reconstitute its power at the intersection of global, regional, transnational and local systems of rule and governance. In this context, it makes more sense to speak about the transformation or reconfiguration of state power than its erosion.

SUMMARY

- The transformationalist account recognizes not only the strategic importance of states but also the changed structural context in which they now operate.
- The reconfiguration of state power does not imply the decline of the state but a more activist, although different, kind of state.
- The command and control state of the Westphalian Ideal has given way to the reflexive or network state.

5 CONCLUSION: FROM THE 'WESTFAILURE' SYSTEM TO MULTI-LAYERED GLOBAL GOVERNANCE

In Section 1 of this chapter four key questions were posed about the contemporary debate about political globalization. In this conclusion, we revisit these questions.

1   Politics *is* becoming globalized and recent decades have witnessed the emergence of new forms of transnational political activity and organization.

2   Global governance is a process of political co-ordination in which the tasks of making and implementing global or transnational rules, or managing trans-border issues, are shared among governments and international and transnational agencies (both public and private), with the object of realizing a common purpose or collectively agreed goals. Three accounts of global governance – inter-nationalist, globalist, transformationalist – seek to explain how governance is conducted, by whom and in whose interests. For transformationalists, these accounts are taken as broadly complementary since together they offer an analysis of both the structural forces and dynamics of political agency that are vital to understanding the nature of global governance.

3   Globalization *does* prefigure a historic power shift from national governments and national electorates to evolving systems of regional and global governance. It also signifies a democratic deficit in so far as the

institutions of global governance and transnational civil society are unrepresentative of the world community.

4   Globalization is associated with a more uncertain and a more unruly world (a global risk society) whose problems can only be addressed by more representative, responsible and responsive global governance.

REFERENCES

Barlow, M. and Clarke, T. (1998) *MAI – The Threat to American Freedom* New York, Stoddart Publishing.

Booth, M. (1996) *Opium – A History,* New York, St. Martins Press.

Darnton, R. (1999) 'The new age of the book', *The New York Review of Books,* XLVI, 59.

Elazar, D.J. (1998) *Constitutionalizing Globalization*, New York, Rowman and Littlefield.

Gillan, A. (1999) *The Guardian*, 6 February 1999, pp.32–2.

Godement, F. (1999) *The Downsizing of Asia,* London, Routledge.

Greider, W. (1997) *One World, Ready or Not – The Manic Logic of Global Capitalism,* New York, Simon Schuster.

Hajnal, P.I. (1999) *The G7/G8 System,* Aldershot, Ashgate.

Held, D. and McGrew, A., Goldblatt, D. and Perraton, J. (1999) *Global Transformations: Politics, Economics and Culture,* Cambridge, Polity.

Kristoff, N. and Wyatt, E. (1999) 'Who sank or swam in the choppy currents of a worlds cash ocean', *New York Times.*

Modelski, G. (1972) *Principles of World Politics*, New York, Free Press.

Rosenau, J. (1990) *Turbulence in World Politics*, Brighton, Harvester Wheatsheaf.

Sandel, M. (1996) *Democracy's Discontent*, Harvard, Harvard University Press.

Scholte, J. A. (1997) 'The globalization of world politics' in Baylis, J. and Smith. S., *The Globalization of World Politics,* Oxford, Oxford University Press.

Taylor, P.J. (1995) 'Beyond containers: internationality, interstateness, interterritoriality', *Progress in Human Geography* 19, 1 March, pp.1–15.

UN Chronicle (1998) p.2, vol.35, no.2.

UNDCP (1997) *World Drugs Report*, Oxford, Oxford University Press.

UNDP (1999) *Globalization with a Human Face – UN Human Development Report 1999*, Oxford, UNDP/Oxford University Press.

Winner, L. (1977) *Autonomous Technology – Technics out of Control as a Theme in Political Thought*, Boston, MIT Press.

Wolf, M. (1999) 'Uncivil society', *The Financial Times*, 1 September, p.14.

FURTHER READING

Giddens, A. (1999) *Runaway World*, London, Profile Books.
This looks at globalization from a strongly globalist perspective.

Held, D. and McGrew, A., Goldblatt, D. and Perraton, J. (1999) *Global Transformations: Politics, Economics and Culture*, Cambridge, Polity.
A historical study of globalization in all its key aspects, from the economic to the cultural.

Keck, M. and Sikkink, K. (1998) *Activists Beyond Borders*, New York, Cornell University Press.
This is very interesting study of the role of transnational citizen diplomacy from the women's movement to human rights campaigners.

Luard, E. (1990) *The Globalization of Politics*, London, Macmillan.
An original and very accessible study of how politics and political power have become globalized with a focus on the institutions of global governance.

Modelski, G. (1972) *Principles of World Politics*, New York, Free Press.
The classic study of globalization and its implications.

Report of the Commission on Global Governance (1995) *Our Global Neighbourhood*, Oxford, Oxford University Press.
A very readable introduction to the work of the institutions of global governance and how they might be reformed.

GLOSSARY OF ACRONYMS

APEC	Asian Pacific Economic Co-operation
EU	European Union
IGO	Intergovernmental organization
ILO	International Labour Organization
IMF	International Monetary Fund
MAI	Multilateral Agreement on Investment
MERCOSUR	South American Common Market
NAFTA	North American Free Trade Agreement
NATO	North Atlantic Treaty Organization
NGO	Non-governmental organization
OECD	Organization for Economic Co-operation and Development
UNDCP	United Nations International Drug Control Programme
UNDP	United Nations Development Programme
WHO	World Heath Organization
WTO	World Trade Organization

Afterword

David Held

There is an intense debate about the nature and meaning of globalization today in the academic community and in the wider world of politics. The debate highlights some of the most fundamental issues of our time. Despite a propensity for exaggeration on all sides, the inter-nationalists, globalists and transformationalists have all contributed important arguments. All positions pose serious questions about the organization of human affairs and the trajectory of global social change. They all raise significant concerns about the nature of political life and, moreover, about some of the key choices societies face now and in the future.

The volume has been organized around a number of questions which were set out in the Introduction. It is useful to recall these:

1   What is globalization? How should it be conceptualized?

2   How distinctive is contemporary globalization in relation to previous eras?

3   What is the impact of globalization on individual political communities and, in particular, on the sovereignty and autonomy of modern nation-states?

4   Does globalization create new patterns of inequality and stratification – in other words, new patterns of winners and losers?

Cutting across these questions, a number of additional considerations are raised repeatedly throughout the volume: to what extent does globalization produce a more uncertain environment for states and societies? And to what extent does globalization structure the choices and kinds of decisions states and societies can make? In short, has globalization created a more risk-laden and constrained environment for governments and citizens? By way of a brief conclusion it is useful to reflect on some of the responses given to these questions in the book, starting with the issue of the nature of globalization.

What is globalization?

Throughout the volume, there is a fault line running between two views. The first can be found in Chapter 1 and is deployed further in Chapters 2 and 4; it revolves around the idea of a fundamentally spatial conception of globalization – the stretching, intensification and speeding up of worldwide patterns of interconnectedness. Globalization, on this account, lies on a spectrum with the local and national at one end, and the regional and global at the other. It is about the stretching of connections, relations and networks between human communities, an increase in the intensity of these and a general speeding up of all these phenomena. In contrast to this position is the view expounded by Bob Kelly and Raia Prokhovnik in Chapter 3. Kelly and Prokhovnik stress that while international trade and investment levels have undoubtedly been increasing in recent years, these do not of themselves constitute globalization. Rather than a global economic system in which there are no borders or other significant obstacles to the activities of transnational corporations, we have an inter-national economic system in which links of trade, production and finance between economies are still subject to the possible controls of states and their agencies. Moreover, key links between national economies still focus on a small group of wealthy states. They conclude, accordingly, that globalization is one of the great myths of our time; we live in an international, not a global, order.

One way of looking at these debates is to identify a difference in the way the term 'globalization' is being used. For globalists and transformationalists, there is a focus on globalization as a set of processes which is altering the spatial form of social activity. They then identify a great deal of evidence of cultural and economic activity and restrictions on the power of states to control events to support their view. For inter-nationalists, there is a focus on the globalists' perceived outcome of the process – a fully developed global system. Inter-nationalists, in contrast, challenge the globalists' perceived outcome to show that the extent of change is limited and that, at present, such a system is far from being extant.

There are arguments for each of these positions, and one needs to be attentive to them. In addition, it is useful to consider whether these different ways of approaching globalization – one yielding an understanding of processes of change over space and time; the other highlighting the nature and limits of these processes when judged against a set model of the global order – might each help illuminate different aspects of the problem of understanding global transformations.

How distinctive is contemporary globalization?

The second set of issues found throughout the volume address the distinctive qualities of contemporary globalization. Clearly, responses to this concern depend on the position taken in the first place about the very nature of globalization. If one is sceptical of the idea of globalization then one will not find it very useful in demarcating different phases or stages of social change. Accordingly, here, too, we find major divisions in the positions taken by the authors of the chapters. Starting with Chapter 3 we may note that Bob Kelly and Raia Prokhovnik set out grounds for raising serious doubts about the strong globalization thesis, that is, the globalist position. For them, the present world, judged in historical terms, remains far from closely integrated. They point out that the actual net flows between major economies are considerably less than a century ago. But they argue that the key test of economic globalization is whether world economic trends confirm the existence of a single global economy. In this respect, they suggest, the evidence falls far short of the overstated claims of many globalists. They argue that the national economy persists, and so does the possibility of national and international economic management.

Chapter 2 also explores reasons for scepticism in regard to strong claims about the degree of change in global patterns of culture and communications today. Here, the case study of the telegraph and the Internet is particularly apposite. Many of the exaggerated claims about the growth of cultural flows and transnational communications patterns fail to take account of how unremarkable certain technological changes may be if judged in historical terms. Many of the claims made about the novelty of the Internet today were made in the late nineteenth century about the invention and growth of the telegraph. This fascinating case study raises questions about the extent to which networks of communication have been altered by the 'information revolution'. The challenge is not simply to affirm that either everything or nothing has changed but, rather, to be precise about what has, and in what ways. Hugh Mackay emphasizes that the scale, intensity, speed and volume of global cultural communications today are unsurpassed. The accelerating diffusion of television, the Internet, satellite and digital technologies has made instant communication possible across vast areas as never before, involving growing numbers of people. But he also stresses that cultural space and cultural systems are more contested than ever and that, accordingly, 'the future is uncertain', dependent on negotiations and conflicts among nation-states, media corporations, technical developments and the preferences of ordinary citizens. Evidence in this account can, therefore, be used to support each of the three competing positions, although the thrust is to reject the more extreme interpretations of globalists and inter-nationalists.

In Chapter 4, Anthony McGrew contrasts the development of the Westphalian system of states and the contemporary system of world politics. In contrast to the development from the late seventeenth century of the states system, in which humankind became organized into discrete territorial political communities, the present period – especially since 1945 – has, McGrew contends, seen a remarkable internationalization of the state and transnationalization of political activity. What is new about the contemporary phase of political activity is the emergence of a distinctive, multi-layered system of global governance and the diffusion of political authority. McGrew argues that this is not to say that all state power is simply being eroded and that the interstate system is in terminal decline. That would be to misunderstand what has happened. What is occurring, he suggests, is an ongoing transformation and reconfiguration of political power. National governments – increasingly sandwiched between global forces and local demands – are reconsidering their roles and functions. States today remain very powerful, if not more powerful than their predecessors in earlier centuries. On fundamental measures of political power – from the ability to raise taxes to the capacity to wage war – many states remain very strong, especially in the OECD world. But they must increasingly work together to pursue the public good – to prevent recession or to protect the environment. And transnational agreements, for example dealing with acid rain or economic crises, will often force national governments to adopt changes in domestic policy. Increasingly, McGrew argues, global politics alter the nature of domestic and international politics, although the exact contours of the changes remain far from clear.

What are we to make of these different accounts of what is distinctive about the contemporary historical period? In the first instance, it is important to stress that we cannot understand globalization as a singular condition or as a linear process. It is best thought of as a multi-dimensional phenomenon involving diverse domains of activity and interaction, including the economic, political, technological, cultural and environmental. Each of these spheres involves different patterns of relations and activity, and before we can make strong claims about globalization we need to dissect what is happening in them. Second, it is clear that a general account of globalization cannot simply 'read off' or project from one domain of activity what has occurred or is likely to occur in another. It is important to build a theory of globalization from an understanding of what is happening in each area. The scepticism of Chapter 3 may be justified in the economic sphere, while different accounts of the nature and dynamics of globalization may be more appropriate to the cultural and political. There is no reason to assume – in fact, it would be quite wrong to do so – that globalization involves a single historical narrative or logic, with all realms moving in sequence. Different processes of globalization may have developed at different times, followed different trajectories and tempos. In order to elaborate an account of globalization, therefore, it is necessary to pursue an examination of the distinctive domains of activity and interaction in and through which global processes can evolve. A full account of globalization can only hope to be built up through these discrete analyses.

What is the impact of globalization?

A third area which dominates discussion in the book is the impact of globalization on the sovereignty and autonomy of nation-states. Here again, not surprisingly, there is a diversity of judgement. The inter-nationalist approach of Chapter 3 holds that the debate about globalization has exaggerated the extent to which the sovereignty and autonomy of nation-states has been eroded. It can be argued, importantly, that such exaggeration can actually handicap the capacity, and undermine the confidence, of policy-makers who have responsibility for creating and administering national economic policy. For a strong globalist position mistakenly attacks the idea that nation-states are still important in the world economy and can manage their own affairs. The national and international economy can still be managed; and states remain major actors in this process. We do not live in a 'runaway world'.

By contrast, the position taken in Chapter 4 differs. It is not that the author thinks that globalization simply leads to the demise of sovereignty and autonomy – far from it. But the overall argument is that there has been a reconfiguration of cultural and political power. As McGrew puts it, the sovereign power and autonomy of national governments is being redefined; the sovereignty and autonomy of national governments is locked into a multi-layered system of governance. In this system, states no longer use sovereignty simply as a legal claim to supreme power but, rather, as a resource to be drawn upon in negotiations with transnational and international agencies and forces. States deploy their sovereignty and autonomy as 'bargaining chips' in multilateral and transnational negotiations, as they collaborate and co-ordinate actions in shifting regional and global networks. The right of most states to rule within circumscribed territories – their sovereignty – is not on the edge of collapse; however, the practical nature of this entitlement – the actual capacity of states to rule – is changing its shape and form. In this account, globalization involves an historic shift in power away from national governments and national electorates toward more complex systems of regional and global governance. As a result, politics is becoming more transnational and global; and the regional and global deployment of political power is becoming a routine feature of a more uncertain and unruly world.

There are significant differences of interpretation and emphasis in the inter-nationalist, globalist and transformationalist accounts of the consequences of globalization for the modern state; and these should not be underestimated. But having said this, all three positions recognize that there has been an expansion of international governance at regional and global levels – from the EU to the WTO – which pose major analytical and normative questions about the changing nature of the world order unfolding at the present time. What kind of world order it is, and might be, and whose interests it serves, and ought to serve, are pressing questions across all perspectives.

Winners and losers?

The fourth area of cross-cutting concerns in the book involves whether or not globalization generates new patterns of power and inequality in the global order. Again, there are differences in emphasis as well as some continuities. Chapter 2 explores the way the dominance of multinational corporations in global cultural networks can threaten the integrity of peripheral cultures and the position of more marginal cultural groups. But the chapter warns against too simplistic a view of this thesis. In the first instance, major cultural and communication flows from the west to the rest of the world do not simply demonstrate power or domination. Flows can be regional as well as global, and flows *per se* tell us little about impact. Further, the cultural products of multinational corporations are not simply passively consumed by people, independently of their position and culture. On the contrary, most people creatively engage with these products; they are made sense of through the lens of local and national cultural resources. There is a creative interface between the diffusion of global media products and their localized appropriation. Moreover, national institutions remain central to public life while national audiences constantly reinterpret foreign products in novel ways. There is, thus, no overwhelming evidence of a simple pattern of cultural imperialism or cultural homogenization in the world. The empirical position – including criss-crossing cultural flows, hybridity and multiculturalism – is more differentiated.

Likewise, Chapter 3 emphasizes that there is a complex pattern of winners and losers emerging in the global economic system. The development of regional trade and investment blocs, particularly the Triad (NAFTA, the EU and Japan), has concentrated economic transactions within and between these areas. The Triad accounts for two-thirds to three-quarters of the world's economic activity, with shifting patterns of resources across each region. However, one element of inequality is particularly apparent: a significant proportion of the world's population remains marginal or excluded from these networks. Recent research findings reinforce this point. Contrast the fact that, over the last four decades, the world's total product (the sum of all gross domestic products or GDPs) has quadrupled and the real per capita world product has doubled, with the fact that a large proportion of humankind hardly participates in the world economic system and economic prosperity. As one author has recently summarized their conditions:

> 1.3 billion persons, that is 22 percent of the world's population, lives below the poverty line ... As a consequence of such severe poverty, 841 million persons (14 percent) are today malnourished; 880 million (15 percent) are without access to health services; one billion (17 percent) are without adequate shelter; 1.3 billion (22 percent) are without access to safe drinking water; two billion (33 percent) are without electricity; and 2.6 billion (43 percent) are without access to sanitation.
>
> (Pogge, 1999, p. 27; see UNDP, 1997)

Kelly and Prokhovnik's account indicates a range of possible interpretations of 'winners and losers' from globalization, ranging from everyone benefiting in the long run to us all being put at risk by international pollution, terrorism and the drugs trade. In particular though, they highlight the particular vulnerabilities that have been identified to the peoples of the poor 'south' from exploitative corporations, the unskilled and semi-skilled manual workers of the 'north' whose jobs may be exported in the search for cheap labour, and women who may become the victims of a global sex trade as well as of exploitative employers.

But the patterns of inequality and stratification which dominate today are not just economic or cultural. Political factors are at play as well. Chapter 4 emphasizes how globalization is creating new forms of political inequality as some states and powers lie at the heart of the contemporary system of regional and global governance and others – essentially those excluded from the G7 and G8 – remain at the edge of involvement. McGrew stresses the way in which the contemporary global order can divide nations, exacerbate inequalities, intensify social exclusion and reinforce cultural clashes. In other words, it can encourage and create a more fragmented and unruly world. He also raises the additional question of in whose interests the new regional and global systems govern; and he implies there is 'a fatal flaw' at the heart of the existing system of multi-layered global governance – namely, its lack of democratic credentials and legitimacy.

The upshot of the analyses found in the chapters of this book on the question of winners and losers in the contemporary world order is that inequalities and stratification patterns are not just economic – profound as these are – but multi-dimensional. That is to say, culture, politics and other social factors interlace with economic factors to produce and reproduce diverse forms of inequalities, major social divisions and conflicts. These phenomena are deeply rooted, with highly complicated origins and pose many serious demands – locally, nationally, regionally and globally. If these and related problems are to be addressed seriously, then politics will have to be rethought in certain respects. For we need to take our established ideas about political equality, social justice and liberty – ideas all rooted in the nation-state and the privileged territorial political community – and refashion these into a coherent political project which is robust enough for a world where power is exercised not just locally and nationally but also on a transnational scale, and where the consequence of political and economic decisions in one community can ramify across the globe. On this matter, there might be some agreement among the book's authors, although the limits of such agreement – concerning many of the details involved – are only too apparent.

Concluding issues

The debate about globalization raises profound questions for the social sciences. There are issues of interpretation, substance and value. Different theoretical positions tend to emphasize a different range of issues in the explication of what globalization means in the world today. The deployment of different theories, and the focus on different domains of activity, can generate different narratives of the complex world before us. But it would be quite wrong to deduce from this that there is simply an irreconcilable clash of perspectives.

The differences among the interpretative frameworks (inter-nationalism, globalism and transformationalism) are important, and they certainly do highlight that 'facts and evidence' don't simply speak for themselves. Facts and evidence have to be interpreted and are made sense of in theoretical schemes. But the foci of these schemes and their marshalled evidence is important to assess as well. The questions that can be raised about the arguments developed in each chapter suggest that we always need to probe critically the coherence, empirical adequacy and comprehensiveness of arguments in social science. For while there are clashes of conceptualization concerning some of the evidence (for instance, how to measure and make sense of trade and finance statistics), these different positions also emphasize the relevance of different kinds of evidence.

For example, inter-nationalists express their scepticism about the whole globalization thesis by laying particular emphasis on the organization of production and trade – stressing how multinational companies, for example, remain rooted in particular nation-states and how marginal changes in trade should not be exaggerated into a new account of the global economic order. Against this, if the focus had been on the changing nature and form of global financial markets, it is conceivable that a different story about the changing growth of financial activity and its impact on the world economic system might have been told. Likewise, we could say that the argument made by Anthony McGrew about the importance of transformations in the world political system gives too little attention to their exact impact on the sovereignty and autonomy of states. For example, it may well be that the sovereignty of states is being reshaped fundamentally in the European Union – where EU law-making directly impinges upon and determines legal and policy outcomes in member states – but it is not clear that similar processes exist outside the EU. The weaknesses in international law and human rights agreements – in particular, their patchy application and enforcement – could tell a different story. The coherence, comprehensiveness and empirical adequacy of theories must always be explored.

But despite the limits and different emphases of the positions set out in this volume, there is also some interesting common ground. Some of this has already been explored above in the discussion of the book's leading questions, I have sought to stress that much can be learned from all sides. A great deal of what has been said is complementary, and offers profound insights into different aspects and problems connected with globalization. Furthermore, it should be noted that all sides would accept that there has been a significant shift in the links and relations among political communities. That is to say, there has been a growth in cultural, economic and political interconnectedness within and among states and regions, albeit with uneven consequences for different countries and locales; that transnational and transborder problems, such as those posed by the regulation of trade or financial flows, have become pressing across the world; that there has been an expansion in the number and role of intergovernmental organizations and international NGOs, and diverse social movements in regional and global affairs; and that existing political mechanisms and institutions, anchored in nation-states, will be insufficient in the future to handle alone the pressing challenges of regional and global problems centred, for instance, on poverty and social justice. What they do not all accept, of course, is the ultimate sense to be made of these points and their many implications.

Finally, it is important to add that the debate about globalization is not simply an academic one. It is also a political debate about the profound transformations going on in the world today. At stake are questions about the ethical and institutional principles which might or should structure the organization of human affairs and the future form of world order (see Held and McGrew, 2000). These questions need to be thought through against a backdrop of change and often of conflict. Irrespective of how it is interpreted exactly, the local, national, regional and global now intermingle in new and complex ways. To this extent, there is a more uncertain and risk-laden environment for citizens and governments – an environment in which new kinds of actors and structures shape, constrain and enable political life. This creates new opportunities and possibilities, as well as the potential for new dangers and risks. The political terrain is being reilluminated.

References

Held, D. and McGrew, A. (2000) *The Global Transformations Reader: An Introduction to the Globalization Debate*, Cambridge, Polity.

Pogge, T. (1999) 'Economic justice and national borders', *Revision*, vol.22, no.2.

UNDP (1997) *United Nations Development Program: Human Development Report*, New York, Oxford University Press.

Acknowledgements

Grateful acknowledgement is made to the following sources for permission to reproduce material in this book.

Chapter 1

Text

Keegan, V. and Barrie, C. (1999) 'Knocking at Gates's heaven', *The Guardian*, 20 March 1999, © Guardian Newspapers Ltd, 1999.

Figures

Figure 1.2: © David Gray/Reuters/Popperfoto; Figure 1.3: © Ravi Shekar/Link Picture Library; Figure 1.4: © Associated Press; Figure 1.9: © DRA/Still Pictures; Figure 1.10: *Financial Times*, 27 November 1999; Figure 1.11: Friedman, J. (1986) *The World City Hypothesis, Development and Change*, vol.17, no.1, January 1986, Blackwell Publishers Ltd; Figure 1.12: adapted from Marshall, B. (1991) *The Real World*, Marshall Editions; Figures 1.13 and 1.14: adapted from Haggett, P. (1990) 'The search', *The Geographer's Art*, Blackwell Publishers Ltd; Figure 1.15: Collection Bauhaus-Archiv, Berlin. Photo: Atelier Schneider © ADAGP Paris and DACS, London 2003.

Chapter 2

Figures

Figure 2.1: *Screen Digest*, October 1996, p.225; Figure 2.2: Mark Edwards/Still Pictures; Figures 2.3 and 2.4: *Screen Digest*, March 1997, pp.57, 59; Figure 2.5: cartoon by Singer from *New Internationalist*, December 1998, © Guardian News Service Ltd; Figure 2.6: Ou Neakiry/Associated Press; Figure 2.7: front cover of Dorfman and Mattelart, *How to Read Donald Duck*, New York, 1975, International General. Courtesy of Ariel Dorfman; Figure 2.8: Jess Hurd/Report Digital; Figure 2.9: from James D. Reid, *The Telegraph in America*, New York, 1886. Courtesy of The Cable and Wireless Porthcurno and Collections Trust.

Tables

Table 2.2: UNESCO (1999) *Statistical Yearbook*, 1999, United Nations Educational, Scientific and Cultural Organization; Table 2.5: adapted from Barker, C. (1997) *Global Television: An Introduction*, Blackwell Publishers; Table 2.6: Sparks, C. (1998) 'Is there a global public sphere?' in Thussu, D.K. (ed.) *Electronic Empires: Global Media and Local Resistance*, Hodder Headline Group; Table 2.7: *Post Courier*, 29 November 1999, Papua New Guinea.

Chapter 3

Figures

Figure 3.4: © Toyota Motor Corp./Associated Press; Figure 3.5: © EPA/PA Photos; Figure 3.6: *The Guardian*, 12 July 1999, © David Simonds; Figure 3.7: © EPA/PA Photos; Figure 3.8: © Sang Tan/Associated Press; Figure 3.10: Institute of Development Studies (1998) 'Asia's Victorian financial crisis', paper presented at the Conference on the East Asian Economic Crisis, University of Sussex, Brighton, 13–14 July 1998, IDS Publications.

Chapter 4

Figures

Figure 4.1: Murdo MacLeod; Figures 4.2, 4.4, 4.6, 4.11, 4.12, 4.13: UNDCP (1997) *World Drugs Report 1997*, Oxford University Press. The United Nations is the author of the original material; Figure 4.5: NewsTeam International Ltd; Figure 4.7: *Yearbook of International Organizations 1993/4*, courtesy of the Union of International Associations; Figure 4.8: adapted with the permission of The Free Press, a division of Simon and Schuster, from *Principles of World Politics* by George Modelski. Copyright © 1972 by The Free Press; Figure 4.9: adapted from Scholte, J.A. (1997) 'The globalization of world politics' in Baylis, J. and Smith, S. (eds) *The Globalization of World Politics*, Oxford University Press. Reprinted by permission of Oxford University Press; Figure 4.10: Stuart Isett/Sygma.

Table

Table 4.1: adapted from Elazar D.J. (1998) *Constitutionalizing Globalization*, Rowman and Littlefield Publishers Inc.

Cover

Image copyright © 1996 PhotoDisc, Inc.

Every effort has been made to trace all copyright owners, but if any have been inadvertently overlooked, the publishers will be pleased to make the necessary arrangements at the first opportunity.

Index